Social Behavior Mapping

Introducing the Social Emotional Chain Reaction

Michelle Garcia Winner

Think Social Publishing, Inc.

Santa Clara, California

www.socialthinking.com

Social Behavior Mapping

Michelle Garcia Winner, MA, CCC-SLP

ISBN: 978-0-97-929220-0

Think Social Publishing, Inc.
404 Saratoga Avenue, Suite 200
Santa Clara, CA 95050
Tel: (408) 557-8595
Fax: (408) 557-8594

This book was printed and bound in the United States by Think, Inc.

TSP is a sole source provider of Social Thinking products in the U.S.
Books may be purchased online at www.socialthinking.com

Acknowledgments

The maps for our original 2007 edition of this book were created by talented therapists at our two Social Thinking clinics in the San Jose area. Thanks go out to Stephanie Madrigal, Sue Day, Randi Dodge, Shelly Henderson, Jaime Rivetts, and Amy Miller for their contributions. Your efforts continue to positively affect the lives of many.

Recommended Teaching & Learning Pathway
for using Social Behavior Mapping

Social Behavior Mapping can be used alongside and to support the teachings found in these core books about Social Thinking®

Described in detail in this book

Lessons for different expected & unexpected behaviors

Many examples of filled out Social Behavior Maps

Tools for Social Behavior Mapping are explored in Social Thinking materials for different age groups

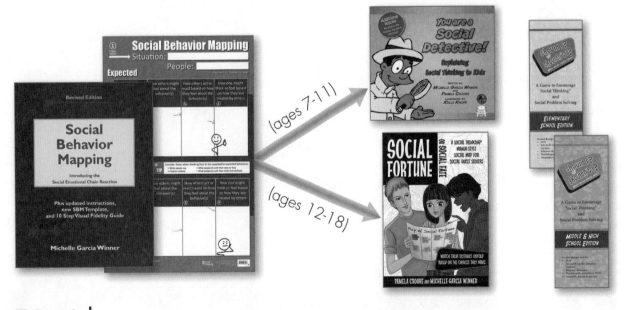

(ages 7-11)

(ages 12-18)

Find these and other books and teaching materials at
www.SocialThinking.com

Contents

Contents

Social Activities – developed by Michelle Garcia Winner

Personal Hygiene – developed by Shelly Henderson Hansen

Contents

Introduction

Social Behavior Mapping
What is it? Teaching it with Fidelity

(Introduction updated April 2019)

This book and the concepts being taught are best suited for use with individuals age 9 and older. Information is provided at the end of this Introduction to explain how to teach parts of this process to children younger than 9 years old.

Social Behavior is a social learning treatment framework that is one part of the larger Social Thinking® Methodology. It has been available to the public since 2002. Since that time, the creators of the Social Thinking® Methodology have evolved best practices when utilizing Social Behavior Maps (SBMs), to encourage that these maps be used constructively to promote social emotional learning, rather than destructively (to place blame and possible punishment on the Doer of the unexpected behavior).

SBMs were initially developed for persons with social learning challenges (e.g., ASD, ADHD, twice exceptional, etc.) to deconstruct and make sense out of an endless array of abstract social landscapes. However, they are now commonly adopted as part of social emotional learning (SEL) with not only students, but adults from all walks of life, around the globe. This tool provides clarity for how we each impact those around us, across an endless array of social contexts. A primary message taught through Social Behavior Mapping is that social behavior is not something produced in isolation. Instead any behavior that is perceived by others is a social behavior. All social behavior is interpreted by others and possibly responded to. How one responds to the "Doer's" behavior may have significant impact on the Doer as well as the responder.

Bottom line is this. Through SBMs we are teaching that each context specific behavior produced by a Doer is likely to influence others' thoughts and feelings, which can then impact how these others react and respond to the Doer in that context. This is then likely to impact, positively or negatively, the Doer's further reaction and response. This process is cyclical, with Doers and responders changing roles quickly, which is why our social behavior is both synergistic and dynamic.

Critical Vocabulary

Social Emotional Chain Reaction
Social Behavior Mapping
Doer

The Social Emotional Chain Reaction is the basis for Social Behavior Mapping. The SECR begins by defining the context, which is both the situation within an environment and what is known about the people in that situation (e.g., teacher, peers, friends, strangers, etc.). The Doer in each SECR is the person(s) who is producing the expected or unexpected behavior in that context. The people in that context interpret what is happening. This results in thoughts and feelings they have about the Doer's behavior, which results in these people's specific responses and/or reactions. How the Doer is responded to by others impacts how the Doer then feels and responds in return. If people are responding to a Doer's expected behavior in that context, their response will most likely be positive. If people are responding to a Doer's unexpected behavior in that context, their response will most likely negative, etc.

We define the contextually based behavior-feelings-reactions sequence as the **Social Emotional Chain Reaction** (SECR), as illustrated below.

Social Emotional Chain Reaction

Situation _____ People _____

Expected 👍   Unexpected 👎
behaviors   behaviors

How the Doer behaves affects how others feel and think

Which affects how these others react and respond

Which affects how the Doer feels, thinks, reacts, etc.

A Social Behavior Map is a visual graphic teaching tool that highlights each aspect of the SECR, with the SECR for expected behavior explored separately from the SECR for unexpected behavior in this one treatment framework.

Traditional teachings, even in the world of social emotional learning, often make assumptions about what individuals already understand about how people co-exist and/or interact across an array of social contexts. It is often assumed children and adults understand the Social Emotional Chain Reaction. Treatment tools within the Social Thinking Methodology purposefully avoid these social emotional assumptions by exploring explicitly many of our more implicit contextually-based social agreements (hidden rules).

Behaviorally-based treatment programs are typically focused on teaching behavior or chains of behaviors without teaching this more complex, abstract social processing embedded in the SECR. When utilizing SBMs to help individuals learn about their own and others' expectations within the SECR, the focus is less on "behaving" and is more about figuring out and learning to participate in the social problem solving process. This process is an integral part of developing social competencies, which is more than teaching social skills. SBMs are designed to teach SECR to foster social accountability more than precise production of specific social behaviors.

SBMs were designed for use in schools, communities, and homes. The goal is to help students (learners in and outside the classroom) focus on learning about the SECR without having to write much language! For this reason the SBM template consists of several columns where students write in single words or short phrases only that best represent the main idea of what they want to convey.

The way we teach Social Behavior Mapping has evolved over time in response to how the community utilized our materials. Initially SBMs were developed to 1) teach students how to "read" the contextually based expectations as they learned about the Social Emotional Chain Reaction; and 2) develop awareness of the production and impact of their own personal expected and unexpected behaviors.

However, we found that most adult interventionists were solely using SBMs to explain to students the mistakes they were making, and at times punishing them for producing unexpected behaviors because "they knew about the expected side of the map but chose not to do it!" As a result, students were becoming averse to any mention of "expected" and "unexpected" behaviors and they certainly did not want to see a SBM!

We now have better ways of explaining how to move through the social learning process with the goal of developing improved social competencies. This goes beyond teaching "good social skills" or "expected/ unexpected behavior." It involves teaching our students through four steps: 1) social attention; 2) social interpretation; 3) social problem solving to make a decision about… 4) how to socially respond. (This four-step process is the cornerstone of our Social Competency Model, which is explained in detail in our free online article, "Social Thinking's Social Competency Model: Attend-Interpret-Problem Solve-Respond (Winner & Crooke, 2017), available at socialthinking.com.)

In this updated version of teaching Social Behavior Mapping, rather than use SBMs to draw attention to individuals' own behavior as the first step and as a means for teaching behavior change, we have found it far more effective to utilize SBMs to increase awareness of the hidden rules in a context that the person is not, at that moment, actively participating. When introducing SBMs, we remove the person from having the role of Doer, to help individuals build stronger social attention and social interpretation in an array of social contexts. Over the last 18 years of using SBMs, we have learned that taking time to teach individuals to figure out their own social expectations for others lays the foundations for them to gradually learn more about their own social self-regulation as part of this larger process of social accountability.

Using the SBM to Explore the SECR: Avoid Focusing on the Student as the Doer

When we introduce SBMs our goal is that individuals become familiar with the Social Emotional Chain Reaction by **starting as observers of the context** (e.g., Social Detective or Social Spy). We actively avoid them being the "doer" of behaviors (whether they are expected or unexpected) and instead put them in the role of only being the observer who is establishing his or her social expectations for the people in this context. When individuals are not at risk for being blamed, scolded or nagged for their unexpected behavior, they can focus on being objective observers to help them learn about the SECR process for both expected and unexpected behaviors.

Learning objectives:

1. Identify the context.

   a. Situation

   b. Identify what is known about the people in the situation

2. Identify the *unexpected behaviors* a Doer(s) may produce in this context.

3. Based on the unexpected behavior, determine the *hidden rules*, which are *expected behaviors* the Doer is to produce. To figure out the expected behaviors, provide pro-social alternatives to the unexpected behavior(s) noted in the earlier step.

4. Identify how the other people in this context might think and feel about the Doer's expected versus unexpected behaviors.

5. Based on the the observer's thoughts and feelings about the expected versus the unexpected behaviors, identify how these others might react and respond.

6. Identify the likely reactions and responses of the Doer(s) for their expected and unexpected behaviors based on how he/she/they has been treated by the observers (as indicated in the earlier boxes on the SBM.)

7. Explain how each box on the SECR for expected and unexpected behavior is related to each other by providing examples of how a Doer's behavior impacted information identified in each of the other three columns.

8. Sum it up by "drawing the map" for the expected and/or unexpected SERC, showing the behavior-thoughts/feelings-reaction connection. Details on how to do this are explained below.

See a sample of a completed SBM and the SBM template at the end of the Introduction.

Instructions

Every SBM has three sections, organized in a way that helps guide our discussions:

1. The Situation and the People

2. The SECR for Expected Behaviors (first row of boxes)

3. The SECR for Unexpected Behaviors (second row of boxes)

(Note there are numbers associated with each section on the SBM. Those numbers align with the 10 steps completed as described below.)

These later two sections each consist of four columns that organize thinking through the SECR:

1. Behavior(s) (expected or unexpected) given the context (situation and people)

2. How others might feel and think about the Doer's behavior(s)

3. How others might act or react to the Doer based on how they feel or think

4. How the Doer might think or feel based on how others treat the Doer

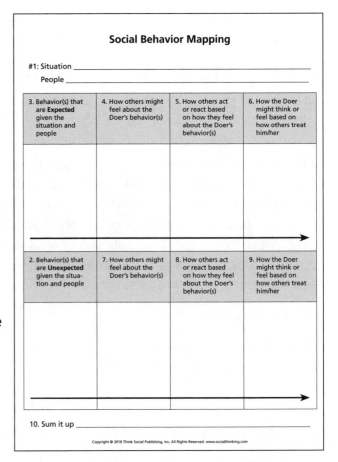

Use the following 10 steps as a guide in introducing SBMs. These 10 steps are also summarized in a chart at the end of this introduction.

Step 1: Identify the Context

Have students note the situation and the people in the situation at the top of the map.

Defining the Situation. The situation is different from the environment. A teacher may be teaching in a classroom (environment), but the classroom has many different situations (e.g., getting ready to learn, teaching/talking time, class discussion time, individual work time, group work time, standing in line, etc.). Virtually every environment has an array of situations. The playground has a vast array of situations, as does our dining rooms at home, the school library may have a lecture going on, quiet reading time, group discussion time, etc.

It is important to note that a situation is never a behavior! If a person is yelling, swearing, getting up from his desk, etc. these are all behaviors that are to be noted in box 2 and not as the Situation!

It takes practice to socially attend and interpret within an environment to practice "reading the situation."

Defining the People. People in a situation may be friends, classmates, unknown peers, teachers, family members, principal, substitute teacher, etc. Figuring out who the people are in the situation is also important as this plays into reading the hidden rules. For example, a 12-year-old telling a disgusting joke to another 12-year-old makes them both laugh, but if a teacher is present the joke may fall flat or get the child in trouble.

It takes practice to socially attend to interpret who the people are in a specific situation. This type of interpretation will always be important when trying to navigate any social scenario, whether using a SBM or not!

Being able to attend to and interpret context directly supports core academic curriculum. Whether students are engaged in reading comprehension of fiction, studying history or social studies, it is important for students to be able to decipher the context (situation and people) for them to comprehend what is happening in the academic texts presented to them. The social mind guides us to interpret information for academic success!

Step 2: Identify the Unexpected Behaviors in that Context

This is the only counterintuitive step in the process of teaching individuals to use SBMs and for this reason, we have added numbers to our SBMs that represent the steps to go through in completing a map.

Look at the blank map and you will see that #1 is identifying the situation and people and #2 is in the bottom left-hand box: "Behaviors that are Unexpected Given the Situation and People." The reason students are asked to fill out the Unexpected Behaviors first is that our brain more easily tunes into these behaviors. Furthermore, these behaviors help students figure out the desired expected behaviors to replace these specific unexpected behaviors!

Have students write in two to four unexpected behaviors they observe or can imagine happening in that specific context.

Step 3: Identify the Expected Behaviors in that Context

Now jump up to #3, the box directly above Unexpected Behaviors labeled "Behaviors that are Expected Given the Situation and People." Have students review the unexpected behaviors they wrote in box 2 and now have them figure out the expected form of these unexpected behaviors. See the filled in SBM at the end of this introduction for examples of expected behaviors written in box 3, based on the unexpected behaviors documented in box 2.

You may choose to include a couple of additional expected behaviors when compared to the list of unexpected behaviors. For example, if a student is blurting out an answer in class (unexpected behavior in box 2), the expected behaviors noted in box 3 may include: 1) Think with eyes to notice who is talking to whom; 2) Raise your hand; and 3) Hold a thought in your head until called on.

Steps 4-9. Completing the SECR for Expected then Unexpected Behaviors

Once box 3 is completed, move from left to right filling out boxes 4, 5 and 6 to compete the Expected SECR. Next go down to the Unexpected SECR and complete boxes 7, 8 and 9.

Notice that the title language describing each of these later three boxes is exactly the same for both Expected and Unexpected SECRs. The words written in each of these three boxes should reflect general emotions and reactions that are experienced and demonstrated based on all the behaviors listed in boxes 2 and 3. Hence, any word written in these boxes could relate to most any behavior noted there.

Completing Boxes 4 and 7 (Others' feelings)

Boxes 4 and 7 are about other people's feelings as they pertain to the Doer's behavior. In these boxes the student should write down feelings expected by people observing the Doer(s). These are usually single words. The emotion words tend to represent positive emotions when on the Expected SECR and negative emotions when on the Unexpected SECR. It is often helpful to have an emotion word bank available to help identify emotion words that are relevant for the context.

Completing Boxes 5 and 8 (How others may react and respond)

We encourage you to have individuals document others' reactions based on the three questions that follow:

1. How did the observer's face or body look (e.g., calm face, happy face, angry face, tight body, relaxed body)?

2. What was the observer's tone of voice (e.g., gentle, angry, loud, calm, etc.)?

3. What did the observer say or do (e.g., gave a compliment, nodded positively, nagged, sent to principal's office, etc.)?

Completing Boxes 6 and 9 (How the Doer may think or feel)

In these two boxes students can imagine how they may feel, think, react and respond based on how the Doer is treated by others in boxes 5 and 8. They can write in this information or ask for help, if they are not sure.

Step 10 *is* Unique

Once all boxes are completed, technically the SBM is complete and the hidden rules as well as the SECR for both the Expected and Unexpected Behaviors in that situation are revealed. Step 10 guides students to recognize the "map" when using the Social Behavior Map.

In the 10th step, after completing their SBM, we ask a student to observe the situation again and then draw a circle around an expected or unexpected behavior noticed. From there the student figures out how others were feeling based on that behavior (draw another circle around the emotion word), then how they reacted or responded (draw another circle) and how the student thinks the Doer felt or reacted (draw another circle in the last column). Connect each circle with a line, and the map goes from left to right to reveal a specific SECR!

Teaching Individuals How to Use SBMs in a Consistent Format

At the end of the Introduction we present a 10-Step Visual Guide. This is a review of the fidelity teaching pathway when guiding your students to complete their own SBM as they learn about the Social Emotional Chain Reaction.

Talking it through the SBM

"Talking it through the map" refers to verbally explaining how we impact each other, without the use of the SBM visual support/template. This can be successfully done at times, only after individuals are very familiar with the SBM template, the progression through the SECR, and have utilized SBMs to figure out the hidden rules across a range of situations.

How to Use SBMs to Teach SECR Across Academic Subjects

The Social Thinking Methodology is not just about helping students learn to observe and self-regulate their social behavior in context. It extends much further. It demonstrates that the social mind is quite active when students need to interpret and respond to educational expectations within the core curriculum. This social-academic connection is explained in the ILAUGH Model of Social Cognition in more detail. (Learn more about the ILAUGH Model in our books, I*nside Out: What Makes a Person with Social Cognitive Deficits Ticks?* and *Why Teach Social Thinking?*; in a free article on our website "Understanding Core Social Thinking Challenges: The ILAUGH Model"; and in our four module eLearning series: *The ILAUGH Model: Exploring Social Thinking & the Social-Academic connection*.)

To follow are some examples of using SBMs to highlight the human experience across various curricula.

Literature

When exploring how characters affect each other in a novel, develop a SBM to analyze how one character's behavior (expected/unexpected) influenced the feelings and related responses of other characters.

History

When teaching history, use a SBM to highlight how the behavior of a country's leader impacted the thoughts, feelings and related reactions or responses of leadership in another country (whether allies or enemies).

Social Studies

When exploring how people in different societies work together, create different SBMs to compare and contrast possible expected/unexpected behaviors when greeting others within a culture (on a single map) and across cultures (compare and contrast SBMs representing different cultures). For instance, the use of gestures and eye-contact varies widely from culture to culture. If you use direct eye contact to greet an American elder of Western European Descent, the elder has fine to good feelings and will likely treat you with respect. However, this same type of greeting would offend those of Japanese or Native American descent. Have students research greetings in difficult cultures and do separate maps for each culture. After the maps are completed, have students discuss why it is important to be aware of cultural sensitivity.

PE

When teaching students how to handle team competition in PE, create a SBM so students can explore what it means to be a good sport (expected behaviors and the related SECR) versus a poor loser (unexpected behaviors and the related SECR).

Group Work

When encouraging peer-group work in science labs or any type of group project, have students create a SBM to explore the expected/unexpected behaviors when engaged in group work. Have the team then complete the rest of the boxes on the SBM to have them study how they impact each other positively or negatively as they work together.

Suggestions for Teaching the SECR to Children Younger Than Age Nine

This book and the concepts being taught are best suited for use with individuals age 9 and older. Developmentally children need to first acquire core thinking and processing abilities that facilitate their ability to work through SBMs and consider the thoughts and feelings of others. These include joint attention, perspective taking, executive functioning skills, seeing the big picture (gestalt) and central coherence (understanding how individual details form a conceptual whole). If you are working with children younger than 9, or children with learning and/or developmental challenges in any of these areas, please adapt the way you teach.

1. Begin by teaching there are expected and unexpected behaviors based on the situation and the people. (Find lessons for doing this in these Social Thinking titles: *We Thinkers!* Volumes 1 & 2 for ages 4-7; *You are a Social Detective* for ages 5+; *Think Social!* for ages 4+.)

2. Next teach that how the Doer behaves affects how others think and feel.

3. Only add the last two columns of the SECR (others' responses and Doer's reaction) if you feel your students are able to process and respond to the first points of teaching.

Learn More About the Social Behavior Mapping Treatment Framework

- The original version of Social Behavior Mapping is described in great detail in my book, *Thinking About YOU Thinking About ME,* 2nd Ed. (2007)

- We offer a free webinar at www.socialthinking.com that describes how to complete our newest version of the SBM: "10 Steps to Teaching Social Behavior Mapping with Fidelity."

- Social Behavior Mapping poster-size templates can be hung on a classroom or home wall and actively used as a visual support when discussing any part of the Social Emotional Chain Reaction. The template is available for purchase at www.socialthinking.com.

Social Behavior Mapping

#1: Situation Listening to the teacher talk

People Classroom peers

3. Behavior(s) that are **Expected** given the situation and people	4. How others might feel about the Doer's behavior(s)	5. How others act or react based on how they feel about the Doer's behavior(s)	6. How the Doer might think or feel based on how others treat him/her
Quiet voice unless sharing information directly related to what the teacher is discussing. Materials only related to class on my desk. Hands only touching materials on my desk. Feet on floor below my desk or on rungs of my chair.	Calm Pleased Happy	Calm face Calm voice Relaxed body	Calm Relaxed

2. Behavior(s) that are **Unexpected** given the situation and people	7. How others might feel about the Doer's behavior(s)	8. How others act or react based on how they feel about the Doer's behavior(s)	9. How the Doer might think or feel based on how others treat him/her
Telling the teacher information about what you did last night Reading a book from home Kicking the chair in front of yours.	Stressed Frustrated	Unhappy face Her eyes look right at you Unhappy sounding voice She tells you what you are doing that is unexpected and she asks you to shop doing that in a loud voice	Stressed Frustrated Angry

10. Sum it up _____

Social Behavior Mapping

#1: Situation _____

People _____

3. Behavior(s) that are **Expected** given the situation and people	4. How others might feel about the Doer's behavior(s)	5. How others act or react based on how they feel about the Doer's behavior(s)	6. How the Doer might think or feel based on how others treat him/her
2. Behavior(s) that are **Unexpected** given the situation and people	7. How others might feel about the Doer's behavior(s)	8. How others act or react based on how they feel about the Doer's behavior(s)	9. How the Doer might think or feel based on how others treat him/her

10. Sum it up _____

Social Behavior Mapping: 10-Step Visual Guide

 = Tips for what to say

PRIME & EXPOSE This is a sort of road map that shows how behaviors affect how people might think, feel, and act. It's a *Social Behavior Map*

#1 Define Situation & People | Generate a situation and define the type of people present. Write it on the map. Go to #2.

#3
Expected behaviors* based on the situation and people. **Write in positive terms*

(Point to box #2)
If [read behaviors 1, 2, 3] are **unexpected** behaviors, then the opposite would be **expected** behaviors. What behaviors might be the opposite?

#4
Connect Expected behaviors to thoughts or feelings to self/others

(Point to box #3)
If a person [read **expected** behaviors 1,2,3], how do you think others might feel? How would you feel?

#5
Connect feelings to possible actions or reactions

(Point to box #4)
So if someone felt [read feelings 1, 2, 3], how might they act or react based on those feelings?

#6
Connect actions or reactions back to feelings (or thoughts)

And then, if someone [read actions/reactions 1, 2, 3 from box #5], how might the person who those (re)actions were directed towards feel?

#2
Unexpected behaviors based on situation and people

So, for [situation] when [people] are around, what are some examples of what someone might do or say that would be **unexpected** behaviors?

#7
Connect Unexpected behaviors to thoughts or feelings self/others

(Point to box #2)
If a person does [read **unexpected** behaviors 1, 2, 3], how do you think others might feel? How would you feel?

#8
Connect feelings to possible actions or reactions

(Point to box #7)
So if someone felt [read feelings 1, 2, 3], how might they act or react based on those feelings?

#9
Connect actions or reactions back to feelings (or thoughts)

And then, if someone [read actions/reactions 1, 2, 3 from box #8], how might the person who those (re)actions were directed towards feel?

#10   Circle & SUM IT UP!

Top of map: So, in **[situation]** with **[people]**, if someone does **[circle 1 expected behavior]** others might feel **[circle 1 feeling]** and they might **[circle 1 action/reaction]** which could make the person who was the focus of those actions feel **[circle 1 feeling]**.
BUT…(Bottom of map) If someone does **[circle 1 unexpected behavior]** others might feel **[circle 1 feeling]** and they might **[circle 1 action/reaction]** which could make the person who was the focus of those actions feel **[circle 1 feeling]**. You've figured out the social emotional chain reaction!

 If the person is unable to generate examples with your tips, prompts, and examples on any step of the map, then stop and teach basic concepts and vocabulary from the Social Thinking Methodology (e.g., attention to situation/people, thoughts and feelings, etc.).

REMINDER: Teach through the perspective of the client as the observer first before teaching about self control or behavior change!

Buy the dry-erase Social Behavior Mapping poster for your classroom or home!

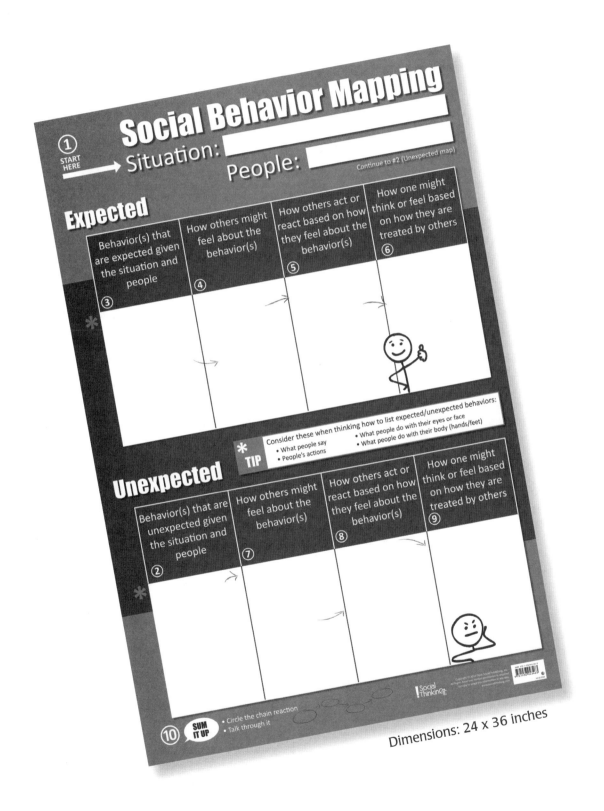

Dimensions: 24 x 36 inches

Available at www.socialthinking.com

Adding the 10 Steps to the Existing SBMs

In adapting the filled in maps that follow to incorporate the 10 steps, use these simple instructions.

1. Write in the numbers 1-9 in the appropriate boxes.
2. Remember to discuss that the situation (Step 1) includes the people in it.
3. Work through each step in the map as outlined previously. You will only be choosing a few examples in each box to discuss.
4. Step 10 can be written in at the bottom of map, or discussed verbally.

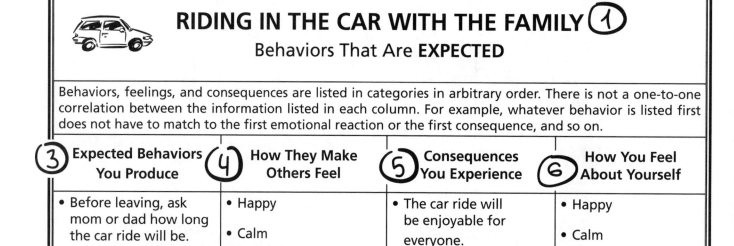

RIDING IN THE CAR WITH THE FAMILY ①
Behaviors That Are EXPECTED

Behaviors, feelings, and consequences are listed in categories in arbitrary order. There is not a one-to-one correlation between the information listed in each column. For example, whatever behavior is listed first does not have to match to the first emotional reaction or the first consequence, and so on.

③ Expected Behaviors You Produce	④ How They Make Others Feel	⑤ Consequences You Experience	⑥ How You Feel About Yourself
• Before leaving, ask mom or dad how long the car ride will be.	• Happy • Calm	• The car ride will be enjoyable for everyone.	• Happy • Calm

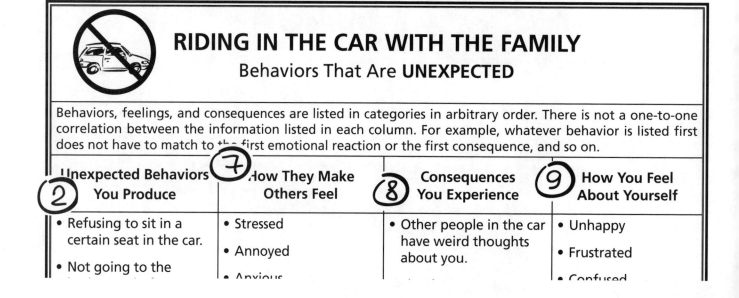

RIDING IN THE CAR WITH THE FAMILY
Behaviors That Are UNEXPECTED

Behaviors, feelings, and consequences are listed in categories in arbitrary order. There is not a one-to-one correlation between the information listed in each column. For example, whatever behavior is listed first does not have to match to the first emotional reaction or the first consequence, and so on.

② Unexpected Behaviors You Produce	⑦ How They Make Others Feel	⑧ Consequences You Experience	⑨ How You Feel About Yourself
• Refusing to sit in a certain seat in the car. • Not going to the	• Stressed • Annoyed • Anxious	• Other people in the car have weird thoughts about you.	• Unhappy • Frustrated • Confused

Social Behavior Maps

Connecting Behavior, Emotions and Consequences
Across the Day

The following pages contain functional examples of SBMs to photocopy and use with children, students, or clients. They cover a wide range of situations at home, school, and in the community.

We've "blown up" each map from one page to two, adding more examples of expected and unexpected behaviors than you would normally see in a completed SBM. For instance, in completing a map users might list just 2-3 expected and unexpected behaviors. On many of the maps that follow you'll see up to 10 behaviors listed. We do this so you can see the potential in using these maps.

RIDING IN THE CAR WITH THE FAMILY
Behaviors That Are **EXPECTED**

Behaviors, feelings, and consequences are listed in categories in arbitrary order. There is not a one-to-one correlation between the information listed in each column. For example, whatever behavior is listed first does not have to match to the first emotional reaction or the first consequence, and so on.

Expected Behaviors You Produce	How They Make Others Feel	Consequences You Experience	How You Feel About Yourself
• Before leaving, ask mom or dad how long the car ride will be. • Before leaving for a long car ride, bring things to entertain yourself. • Go to the bathroom before leaving. • Sometimes you may have to sit in a seat that you don't like. • Keep your hands and feet to yourself. • Talk about topics that are interesting to the whole family – think about others. • Talk calmly to the driver and wait your turn to talk. • If you are eating something, offer to share with others in the car. • Compromise on the music selection and make sure the volume of the music is appropriate.	• Happy • Calm • Relaxed • Appreciated →	• The car ride will be enjoyable for everyone. • The driver can concentrate on driving. • Other people have good thoughts about you. • The driver feels safe. →	• Happy • Calm • Fine with traveling

RIDING IN THE CAR WITH THE FAMILY
Behaviors That Are **UNEXPECTED**

Behaviors, feelings, and consequences are listed in categories in arbitrary order. There is not a one-to-one correlation between the information listed in each column. For example, whatever behavior is listed first does not have to match to the first emotional reaction or the first consequence, and so on.

Unexpected Behaviors You Produce	How They Make Others Feel	Consequences You Experience	How You Feel About Yourself
• Refusing to sit in a certain seat in the car. • Not going to the bathroom before you get in the car. • Commenting over and over again about how bored you are feeling. • Asking mom or dad over and over again how long the drive is going to be. • Touching or invading other people's personal space. • Interrupting or scaring the driver. • Talking about topics that are only interesting to you and not to others in the car. • Using a loud voice or arguing with someone in the car. • Turning the music up loud without asking, or picking music that only you like. • Not bringing anything to do in the car.	• Stressed • Annoyed • Anxious • Unhappy • Irritated • Frustrated → →	• Other people in the car have weird thoughts about you. • The driver can't concentrate on driving. • Other people will not want to sit by you or talk to you. • Other people will not think you are thinking about them. • The driver does not feel safe. • The car ride will be unpleasant. • The driver may pull the car over or end the trip altogether. • You may get yelled at.	• Unhappy • Frustrated • Confused • Stressed • Annoyed

RIDING IN AN AIRPLANE
Behaviors That Are **EXPECTED**

Behaviors, feelings, and consequences are listed in categories in arbitrary order. There is not a one-to-one correlation between the information listed in each column. For example, whatever behavior is listed first does not have to match to the first emotional reaction or the first consequence, and so on.

Expected Behaviors You Produce	How They Make Others Feel	Consequences You Experience	How You Feel About Yourself
• Sit in your assigned seat on the plane, unless the flight attendant asks you to move. • Talk in a low voice. • Keep your seat belt buckled when sitting. • Stay within your own personal space and be aware of other's space next to you. • Say "Excuse me" if you have to go to the bathroom. • Put small bags under your seat. • Only push the Flight Attendant call button in an emergency. • Wait for the person in front of you to move before you enter or exit the plane. • Wait for your aisle's turn to get on and off the plane – use your eyes to think about other people's plans. • Turn off your electronics, cell phone, and games when asked to do so by the flight attendant. • Lean your seat back only if you are sleeping, making sure you are not invading the person's space behind you.	• Calm • Happy • Relaxed • Safe →	• People on the plane have good thoughts about you. • You and the others you are traveling with will enjoy the flight. • Fellow passengers on the plane will think you are thinking about them. • You get your turn to leave or enter the plane in a timely manner. → ☺	• Proud • Excited • Happy to be traveling • Calm

RIDING IN AN AIRPLANE
Behaviors That Are **UNEXPECTED**

Behaviors, feelings, and consequences are listed in categories in arbitrary order. There is not a one-to-one correlation between the information listed in each column. For example, whatever behavior is listed first does not have to match to the first emotional reaction or the first consequence, and so on.

Unexpected Behaviors You Produce	How They Make Others Feel	Consequences You Experience	How You Feel About Yourself
• Sitting in a seat that is not assigned to you. • Talking in a loud voice. • Switching seats without asking the flight attendant or the person with whom you want to switch seats. • Touching or leaning on people next to you. • Refusing to buckle your seat belt. • Pushing the Flight Attendant call button when it is not necessary. • Turning on an electronic device without permission from the crew. • Leaning your seat all the way back without checking behind you to see if you are invading someone's space. • Not saying "Excuse me" to the people seated next to you when getting up to use the bathroom. • Walking in the aisles instead of staying in your seat when the "Fasten Seat Belt" light is turned on. • Pushing your way to the front of the plane when it lands without waiting your turn to exit the plane.	• Annoyed • Angry • Anxious • Scared • Uncomfortable • Stressed →	• People on the plane have weird thoughts about you. • You and the others you are traveling with will not enjoy the flight. • You are asked to leave the plane if it has not taken off because you are causing a disruption. • Someone might bump into you, kick your chair, or move or take your belongings. • Fellow passengers on the plane think you are not thinking about them. →	• Bad • Disturbed • Confused • Uncomfortable • Sad • Frustrated

RIDING ON A SCHOOL BUS
Behaviors That Are **EXPECTED** for Students

Behaviors, feelings, and consequences are listed in categories in arbitrary order. There is not a one-to-one correlation between the information listed in each column. For example, whatever behavior is listed first does not have to match to the first emotional reaction or the first consequence, and so on.

Expected Behaviors You Produce	How They Make Others Feel	Consequences You Experience	How You Feel About Yourself
• Use friendly words and relaxed body language with the driver when getting on and off. • Find an open seat as soon as possible. • Sit next to friends or someone you know. • If you don't know anyone it's okay to sit next to someone you don't know and make a new friend. Avoid sitting next to a person who has been mean to you. • Use a voice volume that is the same as others'. • Remember to take your belongings when you leave the bus. • Keep your body in your own space in your seat; watch out for people in the aisle by keeping your body in your own space. • Get on and off only when the bus comes to a complete stop. • If the bus driver asks students to follow a rule, take care of the bus driver's feelings and follow the expected behaviors for that rule. • Ask social wonder questions to people around you on the bus.	• Calm • Happy • Relaxed • Safe →	• You enjoy your bus ride. • Other people riding the bus have good thoughts about you. • You get to school on time. • Next time you ride the bus people will want to sit next to you. • The bus driver feels safe having you on her bus. • People have friendly, relaxed faces and voices. →	• Calm • Pleased • Relaxed • Happy

RIDING ON A SCHOOL BUS
Behaviors That Are **UNEXPECTED** for Students

Behaviors, feelings, and consequences are listed in categories in arbitrary order. There is not a one-to-one correlation between the information listed in each column. For example, whatever behavior is listed first does not have to match to the first emotional reaction or the first consequence, and so on.

Unexpected Behaviors You Produce	How They Make Others Feel	Consequences You Experience	How You Feel About Yourself
• Using unfriendly words or stressed body language with the bus driver or the other students on the bus. • Sitting alone or away from your friends. • Wandering up and down the aisle when the bus is moving. • Talking in a loud voice or causing noise. • Leaving your belongings on the bus when you arrive at school. • Not following directions or following the rules for riding on the bus. • Talking only about yourself to the students around you. • Invading other people's space or putting your body in the aisle. • Standing up to get off the bus before it stops. • Refusing to sit next to someone. • Throwing objects. • Sitting in an area of the bus with people who are not part of your social group. • Refusing to make room for someone when asked to slide over in your seat.	• Stressed • Unhappy • Angry • Irritated • Frustrated →	• People have unfriendly faces and mean tones of voice. • Other people riding on the bus have weird/bad thoughts about you. • You make other people late for school because the bus driver has to stop the bus and scold you. • Other people on the bus don't want to sit next to you. • The bus driver cannot drive the bus safely. →	• Bad • Stressed • Confused • Uncomfortable • Angry • Frustrated

RIDING ON A PUBLIC BUS
Behaviors That Are EXPECTED

Behaviors, feelings, and consequences are listed in categories in arbitrary order. There is not a one-to-one correlation between the information listed in each column. For example, whatever behavior is listed first does not have to match to the first emotional reaction or the first consequence, and so on.

Expected Behaviors You Produce	How They Make Others Feel	Consequences You Experience	How You Feel About Yourself
• Use a volume of voice that is similar to those around you; usually it is a soft tone of voice. • Give the bus driver as close to exact change for the fare as soon as you get on the bus. The bus driver does not carry change. • Find an open seat as soon as possible. • The disabled seats at the front of the bus are reserved for people with disabilities. You may sit in them until you see someone who has a disability or is very old get on the bus. • There is a line on the floor behind the driver of the bus you must stay behind when talking to the driver. • If there are no open seats on the bus, stand up and hold onto the hand rail. • Keep your body in your own seat and personal space. • Keep an eye on where you are going. If you are not sure where you stop, ask the driver (using a friendly tone of voice) to announce your stop. • Pull the stop cord in plenty of time before your stop to let the bus driver know your plan.	• Calm • Relaxed • Safe →	• Other people riding the bus have good thoughts about you. • You get to reach your destination in a timely manner. • Your experience riding the bus is positive and you want to do it again. • The bus driver feels safe having you on her bus. →	• Proud • Relaxed • Happy • Content • Pleased • Safe

☺

RIDING ON A PUBLIC BUS
Behaviors That Are UNEXPECTED

Behaviors, feelings, and consequences are listed in categories in arbitrary order. There is not a one-to-one correlation between the information listed in each column. For example, whatever behavior is listed first does not have to match to the first emotional reaction or the first consequence, and so on.

Unexpected Behaviors You Produce	How They Make Others Feel	Consequences You Experience	How You Feel About Yourself
• Not paying your full bus fare. • Taking a long time to pick your seat. • Asking someone to move seats when there is an open seat left. • Not moving when someone with a disability or who is old gets on the bus and wants to sit in the disabled section. • Standing too close to the bus driver. • Talking in a loud voice. • Invading other people's space. • Walking up and down the aisle when the bus is moving even though you have an open seat. • Leaving your garbage or belongings on the bus. • Pulling the stop cord and not getting off at the next stop. • Telling the driver in an angry voice that you are lost or that he must tell you your stop.	• Stressed • Angry • Irritated • Frustrated • Unhappy	• Other people riding the bus have weird/bad thoughts about you. • You make the bus late for its route. • You are late reaching your destination. • The driver yells at you or refuses to help you.	• Stressed • Confused • Embarrassed • Frustrated • Unhappy • Unsafe

EATING IN THE SCHOOL CAFETERIA
Behaviors That Are **EXPECTED**

Behaviors, feelings, and consequences are listed in categories in arbitrary order. There is not a one-to-one correlation between the information listed in each column. For example, whatever behavior is listed first does not have to match to the first emotional reaction or the first consequence, and so on.

Expected Behaviors You Produce	How They Make Others Feel	Consequences You Experience	How You Feel About Yourself
• Appropriately stand in line for your food (see SBM for standing in line). • Sit an arm's length away from others. • Sit with friends. Avoid sitting with people who have been mean to you. • Eat your lunch (chew with your mouth closed). • Talk with friends (ask them questions about their interests, make comments, give feedback). • When you're finished with lunch throw away your trash in the trash can. • Hang out with friends (sit with them, talking, etc., even if you have finished eating lunch). • Stay in the lunch area.	• Calm • Comfortable • Relaxed • Happy →	• People are fine being in line with you. • Everyone will be comfortable around you. People are less likely to bump into each other. • People will enjoy eating with you. • You can get to know your friends better; people enjoy hanging out with you. • The area will be clean for the next people who need to use that area. • People will want to be around you. • Teachers will know where you are if they need to find you. → ☺	• Proud • Happy • Comfortable • Calm

EATING IN THE SCHOOL CAFETERIA
Behaviors That Are UNEXPECTED

Behaviors, feelings, and consequences are listed in categories in arbitrary order. There is not a one-to-one correlation between the information listed in each column. For example, whatever behavior is listed first does not have to match to the first emotional reaction or the first consequence, and so on.

Unexpected Behaviors You Produce	How They Make Others Feel	Consequences You Experience	How You Feel About Yourself
• Pushing, fighting, fidgeting, or cutting in the food line. • Running, pushing, or acting wild. • Bumping into others with your tray, playing with your tray, throwing your tray, etc. • Playing with food. • Throwing food or drinks. • Eating with your mouth open. • Telling others how they should behave. • Only talking about yourself. • Refusing to sit with others once you are done eating. • Choosing to sit with people who are mean to you or you don't like.	• Irritated • Angry • Frustrated • Grossed out	• You may be sent to the Principal's office or back to class. • Others will not want to be around you. • Others will not want to sit with you. • Teachers may ask you to go to the Principal's office. • Others will not want to eat lunch around you. • Others may get grossed out or think you are impolite. • Teachers may make you skip lunch recess to pick up trash as a punishment.	• Embarrassed • Nervous • Lonely • Sad • Frustrated

COMPUTER TIME AT SCHOOL
Behaviors That Are **EXPECTED**

Behaviors, feelings, and consequences are listed in categories in arbitrary order. There is not a one-to-one correlation between the information listed in each column. For example, whatever behavior is listed first does not have to match to the first emotional reaction or the first consequence, and so on.

Expected Behaviors You Produce	How They Make Others Feel	Consequences You Experience	How You Feel About Yourself
• Follow classroom rules; if you are unclear about the rules, ASK your teacher or other students. • Some teachers allow you to play computer games until class starts. If this is a rule in your class, play but as soon as class starts (i.e., bell rings, teacher looks ready to work, starts talking, etc.), STOP playing computer games and switch your attention to the lesson. • FOCUS your attention on your computer lesson. (Fight distractions or the urge to play games or work on anything other than your lesson.) • If there is a problem with the computer, ASK your teacher for help. Don't attempt to fix it on your own. • Be respectful of computer equipment. • Be respectful of other people's feelings and knowledge. • You only search on allowable Internet sites.	• Calm • Happy • Focused • Ready to work →	• You can continue to work on computer lessons. • You will get to play a little and to learn the computer lessons your teacher is teaching. • You will get better and faster at using the computer. • The computer equipment will stay in good working order and you will have a computer to use next time. →	• Focused • Happy • Proud • Calm

☺

COMPUTER TIME AT SCHOOL
Behaviors That Are UNEXPECTED

Behaviors, feelings, and consequences are listed in categories in arbitrary order. There is not a one-to-one correlation between the information listed in each column. For example, whatever behavior is listed first does not have to match to the first emotional reaction or the first consequence, and so on.

Unexpected Behaviors You Produce	How They Make Others Feel	Consequences You Experience	How You Feel About Yourself
• Not learning the rules for the class. NOT following the rules. • Playing computer games when you are supposed to be working on a lesson. • Doing random searches without specific permission to do so. • Distracting others OR allowing others to distract you. • Being rough with the computer equipment. • Attempting to fix the computer on your own without permission. • Telling others you are really good on the computer, making them feel like you think you are better than they are.	• Confused • Disappointed • Frustrated • Irritated • Angry • Stressed	• You may be asked to leave the lab. • The teacher may scold you or nag you. • If you look at inappropriate sites, you will be banned from the computer lab and might even have to serve detention. • If you are distracting others, you may be asked to leave. • If you are allowing others to distract you, you will fall behind on your computer lesson. • You might break the computer. • You might not be able to use the computer next time.	• Nervous • Embarrassed • Frustrated • Sad • Upset • Stressed

INITIATING PLAY WITH OTHERS
Behaviors That Are **EXPECTED**

Behaviors, feelings, and consequences are listed in categories in arbitrary order. There is not a one-to-one correlation between the information listed in each column. For example, whatever behavior is listed first does not have to match to the first emotional reaction or the first consequence, and so on.

Expected Behaviors You Produce	How They Make Others Feel	Consequences You Experience	How You Feel About Yourself
• Think about the people you want to play with. See if you can figure out how they feel by looking at their face and body language. Do they look like they want you to play right now? Or should you try again another time? Is the activity full or is there room for you to play? Have they been nice to you before? • Use your eyes to show others you want to be part of their group. • Look at the person or people you want to play with. Observe them. Do they look like they want you to play with them? • Walk up to others and put your body one arm's length away from them. Face your shoulders toward them. • Add your words. Ask if you can play. Make positive comments about the activity. Ask questions about the rules if you don't understand them. • Be flexible. Go along with others' rules (it's just a game). Go with the flow! Be a good sport. You are okay if you lose the game. You remember it is just a game!	• Happy • Great • Understanding • Calm →	• Others will see that you are thinking about them and that will make them feel good. They are likely to invite you to play with them. • When you look at others, you will be able to see how they are feeling and make better guesses about what they are thinking. • Others will know your intentions. They will see that you want to play and they may invite you to play with them. • Others will know what you are thinking and will enjoy being around you. • Everyone will have a good time playing with you. →	• Great • Happy • Proud • Calm • Ecstatic

INITIATING PLAY WITH OTHERS

Behaviors That Are UNEXPECTED

Behaviors, feelings, and consequences are listed in categories in arbitrary order. There is not a one-to-one correlation between the information listed in each column. For example, whatever behavior is listed first does not have to match to the first emotional reaction or the first consequence, and so on.

Unexpected Behaviors You Produce	How They Make Others Feel	Consequences You Experience	How You Feel About Yourself
• Walking up to others and grabbing their ball when you want to play. • Insisting on going first. • Cutting in line. • Yelling at others or pestering them when all you really want to do is play with them. • Not asking people to explain the rules. • Yelling at people and telling them they are not fair. • Not looking at others. • Not appropriately showing others you are thinking about them with your body, eyes, and words. • Choosing to play with people who have been mean to you or who you don't like. • Crying if you lose the game.	• Angry • Confused • Frustrated • Angry	• Teacher may bench you or ask you to stand against the wall. • People will not understand your plan. They will think you are just being mean. They will not ask you to play. • You will miss important information. • People will probably ignore you or, worse, they might tease you. • Students call you names. • People want to fight you.	• Frustrated • Embarrassed • Lonely • Confused • Upset

SILENT READING
Behaviors That Are **EXPECTED**

Behaviors, feelings, and consequences are listed in categories in arbitrary order. There is not a one-to-one correlation between the information listed in each column. For example, whatever behavior is listed first does not have to match to the first emotional reaction or the first consequence, and so on.

Expected Behaviors You Produce	How They Make Others Feel	Consequences You Experience	How You Feel About Yourself
• When the teacher tells you it's time for silent reading, immediately take out your book. (This will prevent the distracting rustling noises that occur when trying to find it after reading has begun.) • Read until your teacher tells you to stop or the timer goes off. • Save your place by using a bookmark. • When silent reading time is over, put away your book immediately (within 10-30 seconds). Get ready for the next lesson. • Read silently so you don't bug others.	• Calm • Happy • Relaxed • Proud of you →	• You will be ready to read and will have more time. • You will become a better reader. You enjoy reading. • You will know where you left off and can continue reading quickly. • By putting your book away quickly, you will be able to get ready for your next lesson quickly. The teacher will not have to nag you. →	• Proud • Happy • Relaxed • Calm

SILENT READING
Behaviors That Are **UNEXPECTED**

Behaviors, feelings, and consequences are listed in categories in arbitrary order. There is not a one-to-one correlation between the information listed in each column. For example, whatever behavior is listed first does not have to match to the first emotional reaction or the first consequence, and so on.

Unexpected Behaviors You Produce	How They Make Others Feel	Consequences You Experience	How You Feel About Yourself
• Forgetting your book at home or in your locker. • Looking for your book in your desk after silent reading time has started. • Distracting others by talking, making noise of any kind, or doing anything other than reading. • Continuing to read your book when silent reading time is over.	• Frustrated • Disappointed • Angry • Nervous • Frustrated	• You may have to read a book that you're not interested in. • You don't get to find out what's going to happen next in your book. • You miss out on time to read. • You bother others by rustling around in your desk. • You may be asked to leave the room. • The teacher will be frustrated with you and may have to nag you to put away your book. • You won't be ready for the next lesson. • You might miss important information.	• Frustrated • Disturbed • Embarrassed • Uncomfortable • Sad • Stressed

PARTICIPATING IN ART CLASS
Behaviors That Are **EXPECTED**

Behaviors, feelings, and consequences are listed in categories in arbitrary order. There is not a one-to-one correlation between the information listed in each column. For example, whatever behavior is listed first does not have to match to the first emotional reaction or the first consequence, and so on.

Expected Behaviors You Produce	How They Make Others Feel	Consequences You Experience	How You Feel About Yourself
• Follow classroom rules and routines. If you are unclear about the rules, ASK your teacher or other students. • Get out ALL necessary materials from the previous day's art project, and continue working on your project or wait for the teacher's instructions. • FOCUS your attention on your art project. (Fight distractions and the urge to chat with friends.) • Ask your teacher for suggestions if you can't think of what to create. • Try to figure out your teacher's plan for the day. • If your project is finished early, avoid talking to or distracting others.	• Calm • Happy • Focused • Able to work →	• You know that you are being a responsible part of the group. • You are ready to work and will have more time to complete your project. • You create a better art project. • You finish ON TIME. • You will be able to work more independently once you know how to get started. →	• Proud • Happy • Creative • Calm

PARTICIPATING IN ART CLASS
Behaviors That Are **UNEXPECTED**

Behaviors, feelings, and consequences are listed in categories in arbitrary order. There is not a one-to-one correlation between the information listed in each column. For example, whatever behavior is listed first does not have to match to the first emotional reaction or the first consequence, and so on.

Unexpected Behaviors You Produce	How They Make Others Feel	Consequences You Experience	How You Feel About Yourself
• Not understanding the class rules. • Breaking the rules. • Walking around class, talking with friends. • Not having the materials you need or not taking them out at the beginning of class. • NOT asking for help or suggestions when you are confused or stuck.	• Annoyed • Frustrated • Impatient • Uncomfortable • Stressed	• You may be asked to leave the class for disrupting others. • The teacher may use his nagging voice with you. • You will not have as much time to work on your project. • Your project may not turn out as nice as you'd like. • You will get more and more frustrated. • You will not be able to finish your art project on time.	• Frustrated • Embarrassed • Uncomfortable • Nervous • Pressured

$\rightarrow$

$\rightarrow$

☹

FREE TIME IN CLASS
Behaviors That Are EXPECTED
(For times when you finish classwork early or the teacher gives you free time)

Behaviors, feelings, and consequences are listed in categories in arbitrary order. There is not a one-to-one correlation between the information listed in each column. For example, whatever behavior is listed first does not have to match to the first emotional reaction or the first consequence, and so on.

Expected Behaviors You Produce	How They Make Others Feel	Consequences You Experience	How You Feel About Yourself
• Ask your teacher what you can do when you've finished your work or when you have free time. • Find something productive to do like finishing unfinished work from this class or other classes, reading a book, or drawing if that's allowed. • Work quietly. • When it's time for the next lesson, put your things away immediately (within a few seconds) and FOCUS on the next lesson.	• Calm • Relaxed • Happy • Proud of you →	• The teacher may praise you for following the rules. • You could finish your homework in class and not have as much to take home. • Others will have good thoughts about you because you got your work done. • You are ready for the next lesson and you will feel good about yourself for having a flexible brain. →	• Proud • Happy • Great • Ready for the next activity • Productive

FREE TIME IN CLASS
Behaviors That Are UNEXPECTED
(For times when you finish classwork early or the teacher gives you free time)

Behaviors, feelings, and consequences are listed in categories in arbitrary order. There is not a one-to-one correlation between the information listed in each column. For example, whatever behavior is listed first does not have to match to the first emotional reaction or the first consequence, and so on.

Unexpected Behaviors You Produce	How They Make Others Feel	Consequences You Experience	How You Feel About Yourself
• Sitting and doing nothing. • Fidgeting with things in your desk or with pencils, paper clips, etc. • Talking to others if this is not a social time. • Distracting others in any way. • Wandering around the classroom.	• Irritated • Frustrated • Distracted • Nervous • Angry	• The teacher may nag you to get to work. • You may be asked to leave the classroom. • The teacher might reprimand you. • Others will be distracted and have weird thoughts about you because they have all learned to stay in their seats.	• Embarrassed • Frustrated • Uncomfortable • Sad • Stressed

UNSCHEDULED TIME, WAITING TIME
Behaviors That Are **EXPECTED**

Behaviors, feelings, and consequences are listed in categories in arbitrary order. There is not a one-to-one correlation between the information listed in each column. For example, whatever behavior is listed first does not have to match to the first emotional reaction or the first consequence, and so on.

Expected Behaviors You Produce	How They Make Others Feel	Consequences You Experience	How You Feel About Yourself
• Work quietly at your desk on homework. • Think with your eyes to see what other students are doing. • Talk quietly with those around you. • Read a book. • Be aware of the teacher's plan, watch to see if her plan changes, like time for class to start.	• Calm • Relaxed • Friendly	• The teacher has good thought about you. • Others can work without being distracted. • The teacher knows you are ready to learn.	• Responsible • Relaxed • Prepared • Ready to work • Productive

→

→

☺

UNSCHEDULED TIME, WAITING TIME
Behaviors That Are UNEXPECTED

Behaviors, feelings, and consequences are listed in categories in arbitrary order. There is not a one-to-one correlation between the information listed in each column. For example, whatever behavior is listed first does not have to match to the first emotional reaction or the first consequence, and so on.

Unexpected Behaviors You Produce	How They Make Others Feel	Consequences You Experience	How You Feel About Yourself
• Repeatedly ask the teacher what you are supposed to be doing. • Wander around the room. • Yell across the room. • Distract those around you. • Get "stuck" on what you are doing and forget to follow the teacher's plan.	• Annoyed • Irritated • Distracted	• The teacher has weird thoughts about you. • Others can't work. • The teacher may tell you to pay attention. • The teacher and students think you aren't paying attention.	• Anxious • Frustrated • Distracted • Unhappy

→

→

☹

DURING RECESS
Behaviors That Are EXPECTED

Behaviors, feelings, and consequences are listed in categories in arbitrary order. There is not a one-to-one correlation between the information listed in each column. For example, whatever behavior is listed first does not have to match to the first emotional reaction or the first consequence, and so on.

Expected Behaviors You Produce	How They Make Others Feel	Consequences You Experience	How You Feel About Yourself
• Follow classroom rules and routines for recess. If you are unclear about the rules, ASK your teacher or another kid. • Line up for recess and WALK out to the playground. • Play with others by thinking about what they want to do and how they feel. • Ask others to play with you. • Use your eyes, brain, and body to observe what others are doing and to show you are thinking about them. • When playing with others, use your words to solve problems or ask an adult to help you. Use problem solving techniques. • Be a good sport during games. BE FLEXIBLE. Remember: sometimes you win and sometimes you lose but you can always be a "winner" if you're a good sport because people will want to play with you again.	• Friendly • Happy • Engaged • Like they are having fun →	• You know that you are being a responsible part of the group. • Everyone gets outside in an organized manner. • People will think you are friendly because you asked them to join you. • If you are using your eyes, body, and brain, people will see that you are part of the group and ask you to play. • You will solve your problems more effectively. You may have fewer problems. • People will want to play with you again. →	• Proud • Happy • Calm • Friendly

☺

DURING RECESS
Behaviors That Are **UNEXPECTED**

Behaviors, feelings, and consequences are listed in categories in arbitrary order. There is not a one-to-one correlation between the information listed in each column. For example, whatever behavior is listed first does not have to match to the first emotional reaction or the first consequence, and so on.

Unexpected Behaviors You Produce	How They Make Others Feel	Consequences You Experience	How You Feel About Yourself
• Not understanding the rules and routines for recess and not asking for help.	• Confused because it's expected that you will learn the rules	• You may be asked to leave the playground.	• Frustrated
• Breaking the rules.	• Frustrated	• The teacher may use her nagging voice with you. May be asked to leave the play area, stand against the wall, etc.	• Embarrassed
• Running, fighting, or throwing things. (You can throw the ball according to the rules of the game.)	• Impatient		• Uncomfortable
	• Annoyed		• Lonely
• Taking a ball that others are playing with.	• Stressed	• People will not want to play with you.	• Sad
• Walking around the playground not playing with others.		• When you are walking around not talking to others, you can't meet others or make friends.	
• Not using your eyes, brain, and body to observe what others are doing so you are not thinking about others.	→	• People may yell at you if you tell them what to do.	
• Being a bad sport during games.			
• Crying about losing or blaming others if you lost.	→		
• Being the "rule police" and telling others what they are doing wrong.			

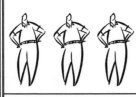

STANDING IN LINE
Behaviors That Are **EXPECTED**

Behaviors, feelings, and consequences are listed in categories in arbitrary order. There is not a one-to-one correlation between the information listed in each column. For example, whatever behavior is listed first does not have to match to the first emotional reaction or the first consequence, and so on.

Expected Behaviors You Produce	How They Make Others Feel	Consequences You Experience	How You Feel About Yourself
• Line up in a straight line. • Stand about one arm's length away from others. • Stand still. Monitor your body to see if you're fidgeting – if so, hold still. • Don't talk (unless you know for sure that it is okay with your teacher). • During fire drills – no talking. • When lined up after recess, it might be okay to talk quietly. • BE ALERT – listen for the teacher's instructions. • Walk together with the class.	• Calm • Comfortable • Happy • Safe	• The teacher may praise you for following the rules. • Everyone is less likely to bump into each other, so you feel calm. • People will want to stand near you. People will want to be around you. • You will be able to hear when the teacher makes announcements. • You will see everything that is going on around you and you will be ready for changes.	• Proud • Comfortable • Confident • Calm

$\rightarrow$

$\rightarrow$

STANDING IN LINE
Behaviors That Are **UNEXPECTED**

Behaviors, feelings, and consequences are listed in categories in arbitrary order. There is not a one-to-one correlation between the information listed in each column. For example, whatever behavior is listed first does not have to match to the first emotional reaction or the first consequence, and so on.

Unexpected Behaviors You Produce	How They Make Others Feel	Consequences You Experience	How You Feel About Yourself
• Standing wherever you want. • Wiggling and fidgeting or twisting in line, getting in others' personal space. • Cutting in line. • Distracting others or allowing others to distract you. • Daydreaming (thinking about whatever you want to think about rather than staying alert and thinking about what others around you are doing). • Not walking together with the class. • Insisting you should go first in the line and getting upset, saying it is "not fair!"	• Confused • Nervous • Angry • Irritated • Stressed	• Others may nag at you to get in line. • People will not want to be near you. • You might bump into others. • Others may fuss at you for not keeping up with the class or holding up the line. • The teacher may use her nagging voice. • You will miss important information going on around you. • You may be sent to the end of the line. • You may be sent to the principal's office. • Kids may tease you for being a crybaby.	• Embarrassed • Uncomfortable • Nervous • Frustrated • Pressured

WAITING FOR CLASS TO START
Behaviors That Are **EXPECTED**

Behaviors, feelings, and consequences are listed in categories in arbitrary order. There is not a one-to-one correlation between the information listed in each column. For example, whatever behavior is listed first does not have to match to the first emotional reaction or the first consequence, and so on.

Expected Behaviors You Produce	How They Make Others Feel	Consequences You Experience	How You Feel About Yourself
• Look on the board at the written schedule. • Take out materials needed. • If you are not sure what to do, look at what other students are doing. • Stay seated, or get up to sharpen your pencil. • Talk quietly with the students sitting around you.	• Calm • Relaxed • Attentive	• Another student may initiate a conversation with you. • People feel you are part of the group.	• Responsible • Relaxed • Prepared • Ready to work

→

→

☺

WAITING FOR CLASS TO START
Behaviors That Are **UNEXPECTED**

Behaviors, feelings, and consequences are listed in categories in arbitrary order. There is not a one-to-one correlation between the information listed in each column. For example, whatever behavior is listed first does not have to match to the first emotional reaction or the first consequence, and so on.

Unexpected Behaviors You Produce	How They Make Others Feel	Consequences You Experience	How You Feel About Yourself
Behaviors • Constantly asking the teacher what to do or what comes next. • Saying you are bored. • Laying your head on your desk. • Wandering around the room. • Talking loudly to yourself or yelling across the room. • Telling kids to be quiet.	• Annoyed • Irritated • Distracted	• The teacher may tell you to sit down. • Others tell you to be quiet. • The teacher thinks you aren't ready to learn. • The teacher and students think you aren't paying attention to the group.	• Anxious • Frustrated • Left out • Distracted

ATTITUDE IN CLASS
Behaviors That Are **EXPECTED**

Behaviors, feelings, and consequences are listed in categories in arbitrary order. There is not a one-to-one correlation between the information listed in each column. For example, whatever behavior is listed first does not have to match to the first emotional reaction or the first consequence, and so on.

Expected Behaviors You Produce	How They Make Others Feel	Consequences You Experience	How You Feel About Yourself
• I get involved in class. I answer at least 1-2 questions the teacher asks or give 1-2 "expected" comments in each class. • I sit up pretty straight at my desk and lean slightly forward during the classes. • I do not get distracted by what other students might do in class. I look at the teacher's face only. If another student is asking or answering a question, I look at them also. • I make sure to talk to the teacher at least once each week either after the class for a minute or two or after school so that he knows that I am trying my best.	• Happy • Relaxed • Pleased →	• The teacher and kids know that I am part of the group in a positive way. • The teacher can tell from my body that I am listening to her. Even though the teacher might not say it, she has good thoughts about me. The others kids do also. • I know more about the material presented in class, and the teacher knows that too. The teacher and the other kids include me as part of the class. • The teacher smiles when he sees me and wants to help me. →	• Proud • Calm because I am part of the class • Happy

☺

ATTITUDE IN CLASS
Behaviors That Are **UNEXPECTED**

Behaviors, feelings, and consequences are listed in categories in arbitrary order. There is not a one-to-one correlation between the information listed in each column. For example, whatever behavior is listed first does not have to match to the first emotional reaction or the first consequence, and so on.

Unexpected Behaviors You Produce	How They Make Others Feel	Consequences You Experience	How You Feel About Yourself
• I do not participate much in my classes. Basically, I don't ask or answer any questions or talk much at all. • I kind of slump down in my seat or move around in my chair a lot. I do not like to sit near the front at all! • I don't look at the teacher much in class. I look down at my "stuff" on my desk or sometimes I get distracted by the other kids in the class and look at them. • I almost never talk to the teacher, even after class to ask for help or to just ask questions about what went on in class. I don't really know what is going on a lot of the time.	• Worried • Weird – especially the other kids • Frustrated $\rightarrow$	• Teachers think I am not listening and don't care, basically. They do not give me good looks. I kind of think they don't like me very much. • Other students think I don't care so they kind of ignore me. • The teachers don't think I am listening to what they are saying. • My parents have to talk to the teachers a lot because I don't do it. The teachers and my parents are upset that I am not part of the team helping myself $\rightarrow$	• Upset • Ignored • Lonely • Confused

INDEPENDENT DESK WORK IN CLASS
Behaviors That Are EXPECTED

Behaviors, feelings, and consequences are listed in categories in arbitrary order. There is not a one-to-one correlation between the information listed in each column. For example, whatever behavior is listed first does not have to match to the first emotional reaction or the first consequence, and so on.

Expected Behaviors You Produce	How They Make Others Feel	Consequences You Experience	How You Feel About Yourself
• Work quietly without distracting those around you. • If you get stuck on part of an assignment, you may be able to work on another part of the task and come back to that part later. • It may be okay occasionally to briefly ask a student around you for help if you are stuck. • Stay seated at your desk. • Ask the teacher for help. • If you finish your work, do something else quietly at your desk like working on other homework or reading a book. • Stay calm and do the work even if you don't like it or you think it is pointless.	• Relaxed • Productive • Helpful • Calm →	• Others can work without being distracted. • Teacher knows you are working. • You can read something you like after you finish your work. • The class considers you as a member of the group. →	• Calm • Proud • Relaxed • Successful

☺

INDEPENDENT DESK WORK IN CLASS
Behaviors That Are **UNEXPECTED**

Behaviors, feelings, and consequences are listed in categories in arbitrary order. There is not a one-to-one correlation between the information listed in each column. For example, whatever behavior is listed first does not have to match to the first emotional reaction or the first consequence, and so on.

Unexpected Behaviors You Produce	How They Make Others Feel	Consequences You Experience	How You Feel About Yourself
• Talk loudly, think out loud.	• Bothered	• Others can't work and may ask you to be quiet.	• Embarrassed
• Getting really anxious if you get stuck on part of an assignment and sitting there without thinking of a way to solve the problem.	• Irritated	• Teacher can't help you because you are not calm enough to listen.	• Frustrated
	• Annoyed		• Lonely
	• Angry	• Others can't work and may ask you to leave them alone.	• Sad
• Constantly asking students around you for help.			
• Constantly asking the teacher to help.		• The teacher asks you to sit down.	
• Wandering around the room.		• The teacher thinks you don't have enough to do.	
• Talking loudly to yourself or yelling across the room.		• You are asked to leave the group or room.	
• Crying.			
• Refusing to do the work because it is "pointless" or "stupid."	→	→	

CLASSROOM PARTICIPATION
Behaviors That Are EXPECTED

Behaviors, feelings, and consequences are listed in categories in arbitrary order. There is not a one-to-one correlation between the information listed in each column. For example, whatever behavior is listed first does not have to match to the first emotional reaction or the first consequence, and so on.

Expected Behaviors You Produce	How They Make Others Feel	Consequences You Experience	How You Feel About Yourself
• I get involved in class. I answer at least 1-2 questions the teacher asks or give 1-2 "expected" comments in each class. • I sit up pretty straight at my desk and lean slightly forward during the classes to show I am paying attention. • I do not get distracted by what other students might do in class. I look at the teacher's face only. If another student is asking or answering a question, I look at that student also. • I make sure to talk to the teacher at least once each week either after the class for a minute or two or after school so that she knows that I am trying my best.	• Pleased • Happy • Relaxed →	• The teacher and kids know that I am part of the group in a positive way. • The teacher can tell from my body that I am listening. Even though the teacher might not say it, he has good thoughts about me. The others kids do, too. • I know more about the material presented in class, and the teacher knows that too. The teacher and the other kids include me as part of the class. • The teacher smiles when she sees me and wants to help me. → ☺	• Proud • Calm because I am part of the class • Pleased • Happy

CLASSROOM PARTICIPATION
Behaviors That Are **UNEXPECTED**

Behaviors, feelings, and consequences are listed in categories in arbitrary order. There is not a one-to-one correlation between the information listed in each column. For example, whatever behavior is listed first does not have to match to the first emotional reaction or the first consequence, and so on.

Unexpected Behaviors You Produce	How They Make Others Feel	Consequences You Experience	How You Feel About Yourself
• I do not participate much in my classes. Basically, I don't ask or answer any questions or talk much at all. • I kind of slump down in my seat or move around in my chair a lot. I do not like to sit near the front at all! • I don't look at the teacher much in class. I look down at my "stuff" on my desk or sometimes I get distracted by the other kids in the class and look at them. • I almost never talk to the teacher, even after class to ask for help or to just ask questions about what went on in class. I don't really know what is going on a lot of the time.	• Worried • Weird – especially the other students • Frustrated	• Teachers think I am not listening and don't care. They do not give me good looks. I kind of think they don't like me very much. They are not friendly. • Other students think I don't care so they kind of ignore me. • The teachers don't think I am listening to what they are saying. • My parents have to talk to my teachers a lot because I don't do it. The teachers and my parents are upset that I am not part of the team helping myself. • Parents and teachers nag me.	• Sad • Ignored • Lonely • Confused

→

→

:(

PARTICIPATING IN CLASS DISCUSSIONS
Behaviors That Are **EXPECTED**

Behaviors, feelings, and consequences are listed in categories in arbitrary order. There is not a one-to-one correlation between the information listed in each column. For example, whatever behavior is listed first does not have to match to the first emotional reaction or the first consequence, and so on.

Expected Behaviors You Produce	How They Make Others Feel	Consequences You Experience	How You Feel About Yourself
• Make comments and ask questions related to the topic being discussed. • Look like you are being an active part of the discussion with your eyes and your body. Turn your body toward the person talking. Look at them to show you are thinking about them. • Gauge your input by how much, on average, the other students are contributing. • Use your "brain filter" if a classmate shares an opinion/view you don't agree with – you may have to keep your thoughts in your head. • Share your thoughts and opinions in a way that isn't offensive to others' views/opinions.	• Interested • Calm • Relaxed • Involved →	• The teacher knows you are paying attention to the topic. • Students know you are thinking about the discussion and listening to them when they talk. • Others appreciate that you are listening to them. →	• Part of the group • Proud • Relaxed • Successful

☺

PARTICIPATING IN CLASS DISCUSSIONS
Behaviors That Are UNEXPECTED

Behaviors, feelings, and consequences are listed in categories in arbitrary order. There is not a one-to-one correlation between the information listed in each column. For example, whatever behavior is listed first does not have to match to the first emotional reaction or the first consequence, and so on.

Unexpected Behaviors You Produce	How They Make Others Feel	Consequences You Experience	How You Feel About Yourself
• Add thoughts/ ask questions that aren't related to the discussion. • Turn your body and eyes away from the group. This looks like you are bored or are thinking about something else. • Give too much input and dominate the discussion, or don't give any input. • Tell other classmates that their ideas or opinions are stupid or that you don't like them. • Share your opinion or idea in an unfriendly tone of voice or state your opinion as fact.	• Confused • Irritated • Annoyed • Hostile	• Others may tell you to be quiet. • The teacher won't include you in the discussion. • Other students don't share their ideas/ opinions with you. • Others may not want you to be in the group.	• Embarrassed • Frustrated • Left out • Anxious • Sad

$\rightarrow$

$\rightarrow$

PLANNING FOR NOTE TAKING
WHEN AND HOW TO DO IT – Behaviors That Are **EXPECTED**

Behaviors, feelings, and consequences are listed in categories in arbitrary order. There is not a one-to-one correlation between the information listed in each column. For example, whatever behavior is listed first does not have to match to the first emotional reaction or the first consequence, and so on.

Expected Behaviors You Produce	How They Make Others Feel	Consequences You Experience	How You Feel About Yourself
• I decide on my "plan" for taking notes. I decide if I'm going to use an outline, "webs," or just short sentence notes. I decide which is the easiest for me to do in class. • I know I need to learn WHAT stuff to write down that is important. I listen to the teacher's clues when he talks. • I always write the stuff down on the board and I ask either the teacher or other students to see their notes so I can learn what is important. • I know that I'm not good at taking notes now. I know that I need help with it to get better. So I talked to the teachers and to my parents about helping me.	• Confident • Proud • Calm →	• My parents, teachers, and kids in my class see that I am trying and they offer to help me learn to take notes. • My parents and some kids in my class practice taking notes with me by reading stuff out loud and seeing if I can tell them the most important stuff. It really helps! • My parents and even some kids I know are teaching me what the "main ideas" are and how they are different from the "details." They are helping me to break down the MONSTER skill of "taking notes" into smaller "bites" that I can chew and learn! →	• Calm • Confident • Relaxed • Proud

☺

PLANNING FOR NOTE TAKING
WHEN AND HOW TO DO IT – Behaviors That Are **UNEXPECTED**

Behaviors, feelings, and consequences are listed in categories in arbitrary order. There is not a one-to-one correlation between the information listed in each column. For example, whatever behavior is listed first does not have to match to the first emotional reaction or the first consequence, and so on.

Unexpected Behaviors You Produce	How They Make Others Feel	Consequences You Experience	How You Feel About Yourself
• I write a few things on my papers in class sometimes, but I don't really have a "plan" for it. • I see other kids writing stuff down, but I don't know WHAT to write… what's important anyway? So I just sit there while they are writing or I just "doodle" on my paper. • No one ever taught me HOW to take notes. All the kids seem to know how to do it. • I don't ask for help usually.	• They think I'm lazy. • They think I'm not interested. • Frustrated	• Your parents get upset and ask, "How are you going to know what to study if you don't have anything written down?" • Other students think you're a loser and don't talk to you much. • Students and teachers see me NOT taking notes and have "weird thoughts" about me in the classes.	• Frustrated • Lonely • Confused • A failure

→

→

TAKING NOTES IN CLASS
Behaviors That Are **EXPECTED**

Behaviors, feelings, and consequences are listed in categories in arbitrary order. There is not a one-to-one correlation between the information listed in each column. For example, whatever behavior is listed first does not have to match to the first emotional reaction or the first consequence, and so on.

Expected Behaviors You Produce	How They Make Others Feel	Consequences You Experience	How You Feel About Yourself
• Write down the main idea instead of every word. • Ask for clarification if the teacher has finished her thought or teaching about the concept and you are confused. • Stay calm if you get behind on your notes; you can fill in the missing Information later. • Work with a good student in your class and copy that student's notes. Compare those notes to your notes. • If you need a lot of clarification, jot a quick note and then ask the teacher before or after class, or during down time. • If you need quick clarification, it may be okay to quickly and quietly ask someone sitting next to you. • Keep your notes in your binder in the proper section. Remind yourself that the extra minute this takes is worth it in the long run.	• Able to work • Calm • Productive • Helpful →	• You remember what the teacher was talking about. • The teacher knows you are paying attention to the topic. • Others can work and focus on the lesson. →	• Good student • Proud • Relaxed • Successful

TAKING NOTES IN CLASS
Behaviors That Are **UNEXPECTED**

Behaviors, feelings, and consequences are listed in categories in arbitrary order. There is not a one-to-one correlation between the information listed in each column. For example, whatever behavior is listed first does not have to match to the first emotional reaction or the first consequence, and so on.

Unexpected Behaviors You Produce	How They Make Others Feel	Consequences You Experience	How You Feel About Yourself
• Try to copy down every word the teacher says. • Repeatedly interrupt the teacher and ask for clarification. • Get really anxious about falling behind on your notes. • Yelling out questions or telling the teacher to slow down. • Repeatedly asking those around you questions, distracting them. • Refuse to use anyone else's notes.	• Annoyed • Irritated • Anxious • Frustrated	• Others are distracted from the lesson. • The teacher may tell you to ask her questions later. • Students may tell you to leave them alone. • You may feel frustrated and rejected.	• Frustrated • Embarrassed • Left out • Anxious • Sad

$\rightarrow$

$\rightarrow$

VISITING THE BATHROOM DURING CLASS
Behaviors That Are **EXPECTED**

Behaviors, feelings, and consequences are listed in categories in arbitrary order. There is not a one-to-one correlation between the information listed in each column. For example, whatever behavior is listed first does not have to match to the first emotional reaction or the first consequence, and so on.

Expected Behaviors You Produce	How They Make Others Feel	Consequences You Experience	How You Feel About Yourself
• Only leave the class to use the bathroom when you really have to go to the bathroom. • Try to remember to go to the bathroom during class breaks or between classes. • Only use the bathroom occasionally during class. • When you ask to go, go directly to the bathroom and return to the classroom quickly. • Quietly leave the classroom. • Quietly re-enter the classroom, quickly joining what other students are doing.	• Able to work • Calm • Productive →	• The teacher knows you are leaving for a reason. • Others can work without being interrupted. • All feel calm that you did not bother anyone. →	• Responsible • Relaxed • Successful

☺

VISITING THE BATHROOM DURING CLASS
Behaviors That Are **UNEXPECTED**

Behaviors, feelings, and consequences are listed in categories in arbitrary order. There is not a one-to-one correlation between the information listed in each column. For example, whatever behavior is listed first does not have to match to the first emotional reaction or the first consequence, and so on.

Unexpected Behaviors You Produce	How They Make Others Feel	Consequences You Experience	How You Feel About Yourself
• Repeatedly leave class to go to the bathroom. • Leave class to go to the bathroom when you are bored or you don't want to do something. • Take a really long time in the bathroom. • Tell the class that you are leaving to use the bathroom. • Re-enter the class in a way that is distracting to the other students (wandering around the room, talking loudly).	• Annoyed • Irritated • Distracted	• Others are distracted from the lesson. • The teacher worries you're missing information. • Students may tell you to leave them alone. • Others don't like being disturbed, so they are not friendly.	• Anxious • Inattentive • Left out

$\rightarrow$

$\rightarrow$

☹

CHOOSING A WORK GROUP IN CLASS
Behaviors That Are EXPECTED

Behaviors, feelings, and consequences are listed in categories in arbitrary order. There is not a one-to-one correlation between the information listed in each column. For example, whatever behavior is listed first does not have to match to the first emotional reaction or the first consequence, and so on.

Expected Behaviors You Produce	How They Make Others Feel	Consequences You Experience	How You Feel About Yourself
• Observe the students in your class each day, decide who looks and acts like people you would feel comfortable working with; also decide who you want to avoid. • Even if it is not group work time, be friendly to the person(s) you think you would want to work with by giving them eye contact, a small smile to greet them when they arrive in class or when you see them walking around school. • Talk to this person(s) socially by asking them what they did last weekend, etc. • When the teacher tells you to find a group, immediately look around and see if the person you are interested in working with is in class. If so, look toward that person and possibly go over to him. Ask, "Want to work together?" • If the person says, "Sorry, I already have a group to work with," look around for another person in the room who you think is okay for you to work with. • If the person says "yes," take a seat near the person and welcome other people to work with you both in the group as well. • Be cool; show all the people in the group you are interested in working with each of them by paying attention to them. • Stay flexible; be prepared to work with anyone. • If you are unsuccessful finding a group, talk to the teacher one day before class. Explain that this is hard for you and you would like the teacher to place you in a good work group before she tells everyone else to go find a group.	• Fine • Calm • Pleased → ☺	• You feel included in the classroom activities. • You feel relieved that you have a group to work with in which you are comfor-table with at least one person in that group. • People are friendly to you. • You enjoy the class and think the students are "cool." →	• Productive • Relaxed • Prepared • Calm • Connected

CHOOSING A WORK GROUP IN CLASS
Behaviors That Are **UNEXPECTED**

Behaviors, feelings, and consequences are listed in categories in arbitrary order. There is not a one-to-one correlation between the information listed in each column. For example, whatever behavior is listed first does not have to match to the first emotional reaction or the first consequence, and so on.

Unexpected Behaviors You Produce	How They Make Others Feel	Consequences You Experience	How You Feel About Yourself
• Fail to notice/observe who is in your class, which means you have failed to consider who might be nice or safe to work with.	• Annoyed • Rejected • Stressed • Disgusted	• People avoid you. • People treat you rudely. • You feel bad about yourself and start to think that everyone in the school is mean. • You think your teacher is a jerk for putting you in this situation.	• Frustrated • Angry • Depressed • Rejected • Uncomfortable • Anxious
• Avoid contact with others. Don't look at people and don't give any positive acknowledgement of others (small smiles).			
• When the teacher tells you to find a group, you just stay in your seat and look at your own materials rather than the other people.			
• Be upset when you are forced into a group of people you don't think are smart or nice.			
• Don't look at people when they approach you to work in the group.	→		
• Refuse to work with the people who approach you or fail to acknowledge they exist by refusing to talk to them.		→	
• Fail to talk to the teacher about how hard it is for you to find a group to work with.			

WORKING IN A SMALL GROUP
Behaviors That Are EXPECTED

Behaviors, feelings, and consequences are listed in categories in arbitrary order. There is not a one-to-one correlation between the information listed in each column. For example, whatever behavior is listed first does not have to match to the first emotional reaction or the first consequence, and so on.

Expected Behaviors You Produce	How They Make Others Feel	Consequences You Experience	How You Feel About Yourself
• Contribute to the group by figuring out the discussion topic. • Go with the flow of the group – some conversation may not relate to the project. About 25% of the time, students enjoy friendly non-work talk. • Monitor your talking so others can contribute equally. • If you don't like someone's ideas, keep this in your head. Possibly suggest another idea without making the person feel bad about his idea. • Keep your body in the group. • Have your eyes tracking the conversation and your body turned toward the person talking. • If you are bored, keep it in your head (others might be bored too). • Work politely with other members of the group even if you don't like them.	• Calm • Productive • Included • Confident • Connected	• Group members work well together. • You and the group make progress on the work. • Group members feel comfortable sharing their ideas. • Group members want to work together again. • You have a final product that reflects all persons' ideas working together.	• Productive • Relaxed • Prepared • Calm • Connected

WORKING IN A SMALL GROUP
Behaviors That Are UNEXPECTED

Behaviors, feelings, and consequences are listed in categories in arbitrary order. There is not a one-to-one correlation between the information listed in each column. For example, whatever behavior is listed first does not have to match to the first emotional reaction or the first consequence, and so on.

Unexpected Behaviors You Produce	How They Make Others Feel	Consequences You Experience	How You Feel About Yourself
• Doing nothing. • Being the "rule police," and keeping everyone constantly on task. • Dominating the conversation with your ideas. • Telling others their ideas are bad/stupid and you don't like them. • Getting up and wandering around the room. • Turning your body away from the group; looking around the room. • Telling the group members you don't want to work with them. • Announcing you are bored.	• Annoyed • Frustrated • Bored • Angry • Hurt →	• Others will think you are bossy or a know-it-all. • They will not want to work with you next time. • They might tell you your ideas are bad and be rude to you. • Others will tell you to sit down. • They will think you don't want to work with the group. • The students don't think you're cool. →	• Anxious • Frustrated • Left out • Sad • Unsuccessful

PREPARING TO LEAVE A CLASS EACH DAY
Behaviors That Are EXPECTED

Behaviors, feelings, and consequences are listed in categories in arbitrary order. There is not a one-to-one correlation between the information listed in each column. For example, whatever behavior is listed first does not have to match to the first emotional reaction or the first consequence, and so on.

Expected Behaviors You Produce	How They Make Others Feel	Consequences You Experience	How You Feel About Yourself
• Thinking, "What is the homework for tonight?" from the time the class begins. • Writing down a homework assignment as soon as I am told what it is and not waiting! • If confused, being sure to ask at least two questions to the teacher in each class about what she is talking about – even making a card to remind me to do that. • Asking the teacher for his e-mail address and writing it in my planner or on that binder for that class the first or second day of that class. Also getting at least two phone numbers of others in the class that "get good grades" and are helpful – I might have to ask the teacher for help with this part. • Knowing that each class is a group and that I have to pay attention with my brain, body, eyes, and words in each class.	• Confident • Pleased • Relaxed $\rightarrow$	• Teachers will be willing to help me because they will see that I am thinking about what I need to do. • Others will see that I am part of the group and think I am an involved student. • Teachers and other students will know that I am interested in learning and will include me and be more likely to want to help me. • Others will treat me more kindly. $\rightarrow$	• Pleased • Confident • Proud

PREPARING TO LEAVE A CLASS EACH DAY
Behaviors That Are **UNEXPECTED**

Behaviors, feelings, and consequences are listed in categories in arbitrary order. There is not a one-to-one correlation between the information listed in each column. For example, whatever behavior is listed first does not have to match to the first emotional reaction or the first consequence, and so on.

Unexpected Behaviors You Produce	How They Make Others Feel	Consequences You Experience	How You Feel About Yourself
• Not thinking about what I need to do for homework until the bell rings to go to the next class. • Not writing down my homework assignment for the next day until the bell has rung, or thinking I "would remember" what to do. • Being confused about what work I was doing or learning in class but not asking for clarification during the class. • Not having the phone numbers/e-mail addresses for other reliable students in my class so that I could call one of them later with questions. • Being unaware of anything but the fact that the class is over for that day and being pretty happy about that fact!	• Irritated • Annoyed • Discouraged • Apathetic	• Teacher may get tired of helping me. • Other students will treat me like I'm stupid. • Students may ignore me. • Teacher may give up on me.	• Overwhelmed • Defeated • Incapable • Sad

TIME BETWEEN CLASSES
Behaviors That Are **EXPECTED**

Behaviors, feelings, and consequences are listed in categories in arbitrary order. There is not a one-to-one correlation between the information listed in each column. For example, whatever behavior is listed first does not have to match to the first emotional reaction or the first consequence, and so on.

Expected Behaviors You Produce	How They Make Others Feel	Consequences You Experience	How You Feel About Yourself
• Observe what is going on around you and who is around you. • Greet your friends or acquaintances. • Use a big greeting the first time you see someone that day. Decrease the size of the greeting as you continue to see the same person throughout the day. • Move your body one arm's length away from others before initiating a conversation. Listen for the topic of the conversation first before adding your thoughts or asking a question.	• Relaxed • Friendly • Happy • Calm →	• The car ride will You won't bump into others. You can anticipate when someone will talk to you. • People think you are friendly. • They will continue to say "hi" to you. • They will want you to be a part of the group. →	• Ready • Pleased • Accepted • Included

☺

TIME BETWEEN CLASSES
Behaviors That Are UNEXPECTED

Behaviors, feelings, and consequences are listed in categories in arbitrary order. There is not a one-to-one correlation between the information listed in each column. For example, whatever behavior is listed first does not have to match to the first emotional reaction or the first consequence, and so on.

Unexpected Behaviors You Produce	How They Make Others Feel	Consequences You Experience	How You Feel About Yourself
• Walking quickly between classes with your head down. • Ignoring people you know when you walk by them. • Repeatedly greeting with big greetings those whom you have already greeted with a big greeting. • Interrupting group conversations in the hallways. • Yelling "hi" across a crowd to someone who is far away from you. • Pushing your way through people because you are totally focused on getting to the next class.	• Angry • Ignored • Irritated • Annoyed	• Students will think you are unfriendly and won't talk to you. • People have weird thoughts about you. • People may talk badly about you to others. • People might think you are clumsy or rude.	• Sad • Stressed • Lonely • Rejected

$\rightarrow$

$\rightarrow$

PREPARING TO GO HOME FROM SCHOOL
Behaviors That Are **EXPECTED**

Behaviors, feelings, and consequences are listed in categories in arbitrary order. There is not a one-to-one correlation between the information listed in each column. For example, whatever behavior is listed first does not have to match to the first emotional reaction or the first consequence, and so on.

Expected Behaviors You Produce	How They Make Others Feel	Consequences You Experience	How You Feel About Yourself
• Putting books together in the same place (cubbie, in desk, under desk). • Looking at Planner to be sure you have materials for homework. • Looking at board before leaving class to write down assignments. • Taking all assignments and related books and supplies home with you.	• The teacher is pleased. • The teacher and your parents are calm. • Your parents are happy.	• The teacher will compliment you. • The teacher will be pleased. • Your parents will be proud. • The teacher and your parents will be more willing to help you IF you need help.	• Calm • Confident • Responsible

$\rightarrow$

$\rightarrow$

☺

PREPARING TO GO HOME FROM SCHOOL
Behaviors That Are UNEXPECTED

Behaviors, feelings, and consequences are listed in categories in arbitrary order. There is not a one-to-one correlation between the information listed in each column. For example, whatever behavior is listed first does not have to match to the first emotional reaction or the first consequence, and so on.

Unexpected Behaviors You Produce	How They Make Others Feel	Consequences You Experience	How You Feel About Yourself
• Putting books in your desk or on the floor without thinking about what to take home. • Not looking at your Planner to check homework assignments. • Leaving class without writing down the assignments. • Leaving class without putting the books and supplies you need for homework into your backpack.	• The teacher is ANNOYED to see books in the wrong place. • The teacher is FRUSTRATED because the information you needed was up on the blackboard all day. • The teacher is disappointed.	• The teacher may make you stay after school to help clean up. • The teacher may not want to help you. • You will not have your homework ready for class the next day. • Your parents are frustrated because you don't have the materials you need to do your homework.	• Embarrassed • Angry, because you think the teacher is mean • Surprised when you get to school the next day and your homework is not done • Anxious and nervous

→

→

KEEPING A POSITIVE ATTITUDE ABOUT SCHOOLWORK AT HOME

Behaviors That Are **EXPECTED**

Behaviors, feelings, and consequences are listed in categories in arbitrary order. There is not a one-to-one correlation between the information listed in each column. For example, whatever behavior is listed first does not have to match to the first emotional reaction or the first consequence, and so on.

Expected Behaviors You Produce	How They Make Others Feel	Consequences You Experience	How You Feel About Yourself
• I know that kids have responsibilities and privileges, just like adults. I made a list of the responsibilities and privileges I LIKE and the ones I do NOT like. I know that I cannot only choose the ones I want. If I do the ones I do not like, I can still have the others! • I worry about things. I made a list of my "most and least" worries. I also made a list of what I can do to keep each of those "worries" away from my brain. If I do those things to keep my worries smaller, I have room in my brain to think about more school work at home! • I learned that lying about homework is not a good idea. My parents find out, and then I get in trouble! Now I make a list of the things I have for homework each afternoon, with the hardest things on the top of the list. It is hard to start with those, but then my reward is doing the easy things last. It's kind of like eating the vegetables at dinner and then having the best part at the end, the dessert!	• Proud • Calm • Happy →	• When my parents see that I am doing things that I do not like to do without arguing, they give me even MORE fun privileges! If I do what is expected for school, they are really loving and generous to me! • My parents like to see me happy so they are in a good mood much more often and even let me have more free time since my work is done! • My parents know that I am in a routine after school now, so they don't seem so stressed out anymore. They talk nicer to each other and to me! →	• Happy • Proud • Relaxed • Successful

KEEPING A POSITIVE ATTITUDE ABOUT SCHOOLWORK AT HOME

Behaviors That Are UNEXPECTED

Behaviors, feelings, and consequences are listed in categories in arbitrary order. There is not a one-to-one correlation between the information listed in each column. For example, whatever behavior is listed first does not have to match to the first emotional reaction or the first consequence, and so on.

Unexpected Behaviors You Produce	How They Make Others Feel	Consequences You Experience	How You Feel About Yourself
• I work hard enough in school and do not like to "ruin" my free time at home by thinking about schoolwork. I deserve time at home to NOT think about or do schoolwork. So that's what I do! • School is so stressful for me, so I don't have any energy at all for MORE work at home. I just want to do what I want to do, not what others want me to do. • I only like to do certain kinds of homework, mostly the "stuff" that is easy for me. Lots of times, I tell my parents I don't have any other work to do. I lie.	• Angry • Frustrated • Worried	• My parents are always bossing me around and telling me to do my homework. • There is a lot of nagging at home. If I don't do my work, there is lots of yelling. I hate it. • My parents do not smile a lot at home. We don't seem to have much fun.	• Annoyed • Angry • Sad

ACTUAL TIME DOING HOMEWORK
Behaviors That Are **EXPECTED**

Behaviors, feelings, and consequences are listed in categories in arbitrary order. There is not a one-to-one correlation between the information listed in each column. For example, whatever behavior is listed first does not have to match to the first emotional reaction or the first consequence, and so on.

Expected Behaviors You Produce	How They Make Others Feel	Consequences You Experience	How You Feel About Yourself
• Each day (Sunday–Thursday at least), I decide what order I will do my homework in and how long each assignment will take (estimated time). I also write in the homework breaks I will take and how long each one will be. Then I know how much time the whole plan will take that day! • Staying up late to do my work just makes me more tired and grumpy the next day, so that did not work very well. Since I am planning how long my homework will take each day, I am finishing it early enough to have some free time before going to bed! • A house has lots of distractions, so I need to do my homework where I will not have "brain interruptions." I will also need to set the time on my desk "time – timer" when I start my first assignment so that I will stay focused and I will also know when my next "brain break" will be because I need them.	• Relaxed • Proud • Calm $\rightarrow$	• I am actually getting my work done at a reasonable time! My parents are thrilled and are giving me lots of praise! • My family is in a much better mood these days because I am being responsible and they are not nagging me all evening about my homework. • My family has time to spend together some evenings and have fun or I have time to spend with my friends because my homework is done more quickly! $\rightarrow$	• Happy • Proud • Relaxed

ACTUAL TIME DOING HOMEWORK
Behaviors That Are UNEXPECTED

Behaviors, feelings, and consequences are listed in categories in arbitrary order. There is not a one-to-one correlation between the information listed in each column. For example, whatever behavior is listed first does not have to match to the first emotional reaction or the first consequence, and so on.

Unexpected Behaviors You Produce	How They Make Others Feel	Consequences You Experience	How You Feel About Yourself
• I do not think about how long my homework will take each day. I do not have a plan for getting it done. If it happens, it happens. • If I don't get my homework done by the time it's time to go to bed, I just don't do it or I stay up as late as I want. • I do my homework in different places, basically wherever I feel like doing it. It doesn't really matter where I do it as long as I get it done. • I cry or have a tantrum because I don't want to do my homework!	• Frustrated • Exhausted • Angry →	• It seems like my parents are always "on my case" about getting my work done! It's not THEIR homework! • My parents are yelling at me to go to bed. They say that they are tired and know I will be tired the next day just like them if I stay up late. • My parents keep telling me that there are too many distractions where I am sitting or lying down to do my homework. →	• Angry • Tired • Frustrated • Failure

☹

STUDYING
Behaviors That Are EXPECTED

Behaviors, feelings, and consequences are listed in categories in arbitrary order. There is not a one-to-one correlation between the information listed in each column. For example, whatever behavior is listed first does not have to match to the first emotional reaction or the first consequence, and so on.

Expected Behaviors You Produce	How They Make Others Feel	Consequences You Experience	How You Feel About Yourself
• I know that doing well on tests IS homework and that I HAVE to put it into my regular homework time. • I know studying takes lots of "brain energy" so I start to study for a test as soon as the teacher tells us it is going to happen. That way, I don't have to study all at once and it is easier! • I do the parts of homework FIRST that are the hardest and I like the LEAST because I get them out of the way – then the rest of the homework is a "piece of cake"! • Since I have trouble writing or do not know HOW to take notes, I arranged to have another student who takes GREAT notes make copies for me each day. Then I review the notes from that day and highlight the important stuff with my highlighter marker.	• Proud • Confident in me • Relaxed • Pleased →	• Teachers know I am doing my best and are more eager to help me, especially since I ask them questions before the tests. • I learn the material better because I learn it in small chunks. My parents and teachers know that I am trying my best to do well. • My parents can see that I am making good choices and they are relaxed and say nice things to me. They are NOT nagging me anymore! • The teachers know that I am not using my trouble with writing as an excuse for not doing well on my tests. They are willing to help me more. →	• Proud • Pleased • Calm • Responsible

STUDYING
Behaviors That Are UNEXPECTED

Behaviors, feelings, and consequences are listed in categories in arbitrary order. There is not a one-to-one correlation between the information listed in each column. For example, whatever behavior is listed first does not have to match to the first emotional reaction or the first consequence, and so on.

Unexpected Behaviors You Produce	How They Make Others Feel	Consequences You Experience	How You Feel About Yourself
• I do not consider studying as part of "homework" so I don't plan for it. • I either study the night before or the morning of most of my tests. • I put off studying for tests because I just hate it! • I don't take notes on what I read in my books (takes too long or I have lots of trouble with writing), so I don't really have anything to study when I have a test. • I think I remember everything. No need to study.	• Frustrated • Annoyed • Disappointed • Worried	• Poor test grades so teachers feel I am not learning and they are not doing a good job of teaching. • My grades are poor or are lower than I am capable of so parents are nagging me about tests all the time. • Teachers tell me that I WAS taught how to study and my parents say the same thing. They don't know why I didn't learn it. • Fellow students know that I am not doing so well in the classes and may look at me as someone who doesn't care about school very much.	• Disappointed in myself • Stupid • Frustrated

→

→

TALKING TO FRIENDS ON YOUR CELL PHONE
Behaviors That Are **EXPECTED**

Behaviors, feelings, and consequences are listed in categories in arbitrary order. There is not a one-to-one correlation between the information listed in each column. For example, whatever behavior is listed first does not have to match to the first emotional reaction or the first consequence, and so on.

Expected Behaviors You Produce	How They Make Others Feel	Consequences You Experience	How You Feel About Yourself
• Put away your cell phone with personal possessions during class. • Make calls only when it is acceptable to do so at school. Check with other kids to figure out the rules. Many schools tell you cell phones are not allowed, but they allow students to use them during breaks. The stated rules may not be the real rules! • Call a person to show you are interested in them. Ask them about their day, find out what their plans are for the weekend, ask if they want to get together to "hang out." • Call people back if they have called you. • Call people to clarify homework assignments, even if you do not know the person well. • If you call people for help, also make sure you "chat" with them, ask them about their day, and be sure you thank them for their help. • Avoid using your cell phone when in restaurants.	• Calm • Friendly • Happy • Helpful →	• People are friendly since you have shown you are interested in them. • People may give you a call back. • People have a nice tone in their voice. • People may call you to ask for help. →	• Pleased • Calm • Included • Happy

TALKING TO FRIENDS ON YOUR CELL PHONE
Behaviors That Are **UNEXPECTED**

Behaviors, feelings, and consequences are listed in categories in arbitrary order. There is not a one-to-one correlation between the information listed in each column. For example, whatever behavior is listed first does not have to match to the first emotional reaction or the first consequence, and so on.

Unexpected Behaviors You Produce	How They Make Others Feel	Consequences You Experience	How You Feel About Yourself
• Cell phone is out on the desk during class. • Making or receiving calls during class time or during times at school when you are not allowed to do so. • Calling people over and over again, even if they don't return your calls or tell you they are too busy to talk when you call them. (They are indirectly trying to tell you they don't want to talk.) • Not calling classmates to ask for help or clarification on an assignment, especially when you are part of a group project. • Calling friends to talk when with family at restaurants or on family outings. • Refusing to call a person who has called you only because you are too anxious to talk on the phone.	• Teachers are angry or frustrated. • Annoyed • Irritated • Worried about your intentions • Angry	• Angry words, angry faces, from adults in class. • People may ignore you. • Angry face when you see the person you were calling too much. • People may talk badly about you to others, or tell others you are stalking or harassing them. • Receiving angry calls back. • People don't call you back at all..	• Sad • Angry • Stressed • Not included • Upset

→

→

SENDING TEXT MESSAGES
Behaviors That Are **EXPECTED**

Behaviors, feelings, and consequences are listed in categories in arbitrary order. There is not a one-to-one correlation between the information listed in each column. For example, whatever behavior is listed first does not have to match to the first emotional reaction or the first consequence, and so on.

Expected Behaviors You Produce	How They Make Others Feel	Consequences You Experience	How You Feel About Yourself
• Cell phone is put away with personal possessions during class. • Send text messages only when it is acceptable to do so at school. Check with other kids to figure out the rules. Many schools tell you cell phones are not allowed, but they allow students to use them during breaks. The stated rules may not be the real rules! • Text a person to show you are interested in him. Ask him about his day, find out what his plans are for the weekend, ask if he wants to get together to "hang out." • Call a person back if she has called you. • Text a variety of messages. • Text a person one or two times. If he does not reply, stop texting him. • Not texting friends when on family outings or dinners.	• Calm • Friendly • Happy →	• The teacher uses friendly voice, words, and face. • People are friendly since you have shown you are interested in them. • Friends respond positively to your text message. • Friends initiate text messages to you, showing interest in you. →	• Happy • Pleased • Accepted • Included

SENDING TEXT MESSAGES
Behaviors That Are UNEXPECTED

Behaviors, feelings, and consequences are listed in categories in arbitrary order. There is not a one-to-one correlation between the information listed in each column. For example, whatever behavior is listed first does not have to match to the first emotional reaction or the first consequence, and so on.

Unexpected Behaviors You Produce	How They Make Others Feel	Consequences You Experience	How You Feel About Yourself
• Sending text messages during classroom time. • Constantly texting the same person, even though she is not responding. (She is indirectly trying to tell you she doesn't want to text with you.) • Asking the same question in each text. • Sending text messages in the middle of the night when you are not sure of others' sleeping habits. • Texting friends during family meals or outings.	• Teachers are angry or frustrated. • Annoyed • Irritated • Worried about your intentions • Mad	• Angry words, angry face from the teacher. • Angry face when you see the person who you have been sending too many text messages to. • The person may ignore you. • The person may talk badly about you to others, or tell others you are stalking or harassing him. • You may receive an angry text back. • People don't text you back at all.	• Sad • Stressed • Mad • Excluded • Rejected

→

→

☹

CHAT ROOM SAFETY ON THE INTERNET
Behaviors That Are EXPECTED

Behaviors, feelings, and consequences are listed in categories in arbitrary order. There is not a one-to-one correlation between the information listed in each column. For example, whatever behavior is listed first does not have to match to the first emotional reaction or the first consequence, and so on.

Expected Behaviors You Produce	How They Make Others Feel	Consequences You Experience	How You Feel About Yourself
• Only discuss the topic of the chatroom. • Avoid sharing any personal information. • Avoid talking to the person on the phone or through e-mail, or text message away from the chatroom. • Do not send photos of yourself on the web. • Do not share any information about your family or your pets. • Do not give out your address, phone number, school name, directions to your house, or the name of the city you live in.	• Happy to discuss the chatroom topic • Feel you can be trusted • Recognize you respect boundaries • Safe →	• People in chatroom talk to you only about the topic. • Others recognize that your personal information is private. • Safety →	• Calm • Pleased to have a new chat friend • Happy

☺

CHAT ROOM SAFETY ON THE INTERNET
Behaviors That Are **UNEXPECTED**

Behaviors, feelings, and consequences are listed in categories in arbitrary order. There is not a one-to-one correlation between the information listed in each column. For example, whatever behavior is listed first does not have to match to the first emotional reaction or the first consequence, and so on.

Unexpected Behaviors You Produce	How They Make Others Feel	Consequences You Experience	How You Feel About Yourself
• Tell people your real first and last name. • Tell people your address or phone number. • Give out personal information about your life and family. • Agree to show pictures of yourself if asked. • Agree to send video of yourself, or take your clothes off for the person on video. • Meet with others from a chatroom in person.	• Person feels you are naïve. • Person thinks they can easily manipulate you. • Person may feel they may be able to steal from you. • Person may feel they may be able to engage you in sexual acts. • Person feels you are naïve, you can easily be manipulated, may feel you want to engage in sexual acts, and they may kidnap you.	• Person may steal from you or your family. • Person may start out friendly, then change to being mean as he gets you to do more for him. • Person may steal from you, may blackmail you or may rape you. • Person may use your picture or video to masturbate with. • Person may post your picture or video on the internet for others to see.	• Angry • Sad • Scared • Stressed • Abused • Embarrassed

→

→

☹

VISITING ANOTHER PERSON'S HOUSE
Behaviors That Are EXPECTED

Behaviors, feelings, and consequences are listed in categories in arbitrary order. There is not a one-to-one correlation between the information listed in each column. For example, whatever behavior is listed first does not have to match to the first emotional reaction or the first consequence, and so on.

Expected Behaviors You Produce	How They Make Others Feel	Consequences You Experience	How You Feel About Yourself
• Ring the doorbell or knock on the door and wait until someone opens the door, even if you know your friend is inside. • Greet the person who opens the door, ask politely if your friend is home, even if you know she is. • Greet your friend. • Acknowledge the other people there by looking at them and smiling or greeting them. • Follow your friend to the part of the house she takes you to. • Stay with your friend in the house; don't wander around without your friend. • Ask to use the bathroom and then ask where it is. (This lets your friend know your intentions.) • Clean up after yourself in the bathroom. • Feel free to tell your friend what you like to do, but avoid insisting on what you want. • Upon leaving the house, say thank you to the parents for having you over.	• Calm • Friendly • Happy • Safe →	• People are friendly since you have shown that you are interested in them. • Other people welcome you to the house and treat you politely. • People have a nice tone in their voice. • You enjoy being included and sharing your activities with a friend. • Your friend becomes a better friend since you show you are thinking about her. • The friend wants to hang out with you again in the future. • The parents think you are nice and polite and encourage their child to hang out with you again.. →	• Calm • Pleased • Happy • Included

VISITING ANOTHER PERSON'S HOUSE
Behaviors That Are **UNEXPECTED**

Behaviors, feelings, and consequences are listed in categories in arbitrary order. There is not a one-to-one correlation between the information listed in each column. For example, whatever behavior is listed first does not have to match to the first emotional reaction or the first consequence, and so on.

Unexpected Behaviors You Produce	How They Make Others Feel	Consequences You Experience	How You Feel About Yourself
• Walk directly into the house without ringing the doorbell or knocking. • Fail to acknowledge the person who is at the door, just walk in when the door is opened. • Fail to greet your friend and just start saying what you want to do. • Refuse to acknowledge anyone else in the house while you are walking through. • Go into a room of interest to you, even if it is not the room your friend is going to. • Wander around the house once your friend starts using the computer. • Don't ask to use the bathroom, just wander around looking for it. • Leave a mess in the bathroom. • Don't thank the parents if they are home. • Walk out of the house to leave with saying goodbye.	• Annoyed • Upset • Hurt • Mad • Disgusted • Offended →	• YIrritated words, angry faces from grown-ups in the house. • Your friend and the parents may want you to leave soon. • Your friend may talk badly about you to others or tell others you are selfish. • Your friend may ignore you in the future. • The parents will think you have bad manners. • The parents may not want you to come over anymore to see your friend. →	• Upset • Sad • Lonely • Stressed • Embarrassed

WHEN FRIENDS VISIT YOUR HOUSE
Behaviors That Are EXPECTED

Behaviors, feelings, and consequences are listed in categories in arbitrary order. There is not a one-to-one correlation between the information listed in each column. For example, whatever behavior is listed first does not have to match to the first emotional reaction or the first consequence, and so on.

Expected Behaviors You Produce	How They Make Others Feel	Consequences You Experience	How You Feel About Yourself
• When they come to your front door, get up from what you are doing and greet them. • Introduce them to your parents or whoever else is home (so no one thinks there is a stranger in the house). • Ask them what they want to do. • If you are playing games, give your visitors an opportunity to play and a choice in what is being played. • If they don't want to do what you want to do, work out a different choice and remember it is nice to have someone to be with even if the situation is not perfect for you. • Offer them a snack or drink, especially if you are eating or drinking. • Stay with them while they are in your house. • Avoid talking to other friends on the phone and telling the other friends that you are "bored" or wish they could come over while the other friend is sitting there listening.	• Welcome • Friendly • Happy • Safe	• People are friendly since you have shown that you are interested in them. • Other people welcome your friend to the house and treat them politely. • People have a nice tone in their voice. • You enjoy being included and sharing activities with a friend. • Your friend becomes a better friend since you show you are thinking about them. • The friend wants to hang out with you again in the future. • Your parents give you some space to just enjoy time with your friend.	• Happy • Pleased • Calm • Included

$\rightarrow$

$\rightarrow$

☺

WHEN FRIENDS VISIT YOUR HOUSE
Behaviors That Are UNEXPECTED

Behaviors, feelings, and consequences are listed in categories in arbitrary order. There is not a one-to-one correlation between the information listed in each column. For example, whatever behavior is listed first does not have to match to the first emotional reaction or the first consequence, and so on.

Unexpected Behaviors You Produce	How They Make Others Feel	Consequences You Experience	How You Feel About Yourself
• Don't greet your friends, and make them find you in your house. • Don't introduce your friends to anyone else, so everyone is wondering who they are. • Tell your friends what they will do when they are at your house. • Have them watch you while you play computer games or engage in your hobby. • If they say they want to do something else, you just ignore them or say "no." • You don't offer them anything to eat or drink, even if you are eating and drinking. • Let them wander around your house while you continue to do what is fun for you.	• Frustrated • Embarrassed • Hurt • Mad • Offended	• Angry words, angry faces from your friends. • Your friends may want to leave soon after they got there. • Your friends may talk badly about you to others or tell others you are selfish. • Your friends may ignore you in the future. • Your friends may not return your phone calls. • Your parents may tell you that you should be doing more with those friends.	• Sad • Mad • Stressed • Alone • Upset

AT A SCHOOL DANCE
Behaviors That Are **EXPECTED**

Behaviors, feelings, and consequences are listed in categories in arbitrary order. There is not a one-to-one correlation between the information listed in each column. For example, whatever behavior is listed first does not have to match to the first emotional reaction or the first consequence, and so on.

Expected Behaviors You Produce	How They Make Others Feel	Consequences You Experience	How You Feel About Yourself
• Initiate friendly greetings to others, even people you are close friends with. • Ignore it if you don't like the music. Avoid complaining. • Do not feel you must dance with only one person – groups often dance together. • Join into groups and talk about what the group is talking about. Add related comments. • Do not play/bring handheld video games – this is a time to engage with other people. • Avoid dancing by yourself. • If you've asked a person to dance two times, and the person has turned you down both times, don't ask that person again.	• Friendly • Satisfied • Happy • Included →	• People acknowledge you positively. • People dance with you. • People talk to you. • People may ask you to dance. →	• Happy • Pleased • Calm • Included

☺

AT A SCHOOL DANCE
Behaviors That Are **UNEXPECTED**

Behaviors, feelings, and consequences are listed in categories in arbitrary order. There is not a one-to-one correlation between the information listed in each column. For example, whatever behavior is listed first does not have to match to the first emotional reaction or the first consequence, and so on.

Unexpected Behaviors You Produce	How They Make Others Feel	Consequences You Experience	How You Feel About Yourself
• Complaining constantly about the music selection. • Dancing by yourself all night. • Standing by yourself next to the wall. • Looking miserable or bored. • Playing hand-held games. • Asking the same person to dance over and over again, even though the person keeps telling you she is tired, busy, etc. • Screaming because the music is too loud.	• Irritated • Uncomfortable • Upset • Unfriendly • Offended	• People will not want to be with you. • People talk about you because they are having a "weird thought." • People will not come to talk to you or ask you to dance with them. • People look at you with unhappy faces.	• Annoyed • Hurt • Sad • Lonely • Upset

IF YOU HAVE ACNE
Behaviors That Are EXPECTED

Behaviors, feelings, and consequences are listed in categories in arbitrary order. There is not a one-to-one correlation between the information listed in each column. For example, whatever behavior is listed first does not have to match to the first emotional reaction or the first consequence, and so on.

Expected Behaviors You Produce	How They Make Others Feel	Consequences You Experience	How You Feel About Yourself
• Wash your face once in the morning and once in the evening before bed. • Do not pop pimples. • Do not pick pimples. • Do not scratch pimples. • Ask your doctor to prescribe medicine. • Eat healthy foods. • Drink plenty of water.	• Calm • Happy • Proud • Comfortable	• Your parents do not nag you. • People are not embarrassed to hang out with you. • People are proud to be your friend. • Others do not yell at you to stop touching your pimples. • People will not call you names because your pimples will go away. • Others will have fine thoughts about your face care. Basically people don't notice.	• Happy • Clean • Calm • Connected

→

→

☺

IF YOU HAVE ACNE
Behaviors That Are **UNEXPECTED**

Behaviors, feelings, and consequences are listed in categories in arbitrary order. There is not a one-to-one correlation between the information listed in each column. For example, whatever behavior is listed first does not have to match to the first emotional reaction or the first consequence, and so on.

Unexpected Behaviors You Produce	How They Make Others Feel	Consequences You Experience	How You Feel About Yourself
• Do not wash your face. • Do not apply acne medicine. • Pick at your pimples. • Pop your pimples. • Scratch your pimples. • Eat foods that are high in fat such as fried foods.	• Grossed out • Surprised • Embarrassed • Unfriendly	• Your parents will nag you to wash your face. • Others will tell you that you should use medicine, or they will think it. • Others will be embarrassed to hang out with you. • Others may call you names. • Others may tell you that you should eat healthier foods. • You end up with facial scars.	• Mad • Embarrassed • Frustrated • Sad • Left out • Scarred

→

→

☹

COMBING/BRUSHING YOUR HAIR
Behaviors That Are **EXPECTED**

Behaviors, feelings, and consequences are listed in categories in arbitrary order. There is not a one-to-one correlation between the information listed in each column. For example, whatever behavior is listed first does not have to match to the first emotional reaction or the first consequence, and so on.

Expected Behaviors You Produce	How They Make Others Feel	Consequences You Experience	How You Feel About Yourself
• Comb or brush hair every morning in your bedroom or bathroom. • Avoid combing your hair around food or in cooking or dining areas. • Comb or brush hair after you wash it. • Look in a mirror to see if your hair looks cared for. • If you take your hat off you should comb your hair. • Do not share combs or brushes with other people. • It is best to comb or brush hair in privacy.	• Pleased • Happy • Impressed • Grateful →	• Others will say nice words like "your hair looks nice." • People will not yell at you for getting hair in the food. • Your hair will look good. • You will not get someone else's dandruff. • People will not have weird thoughts about your hair. →	• Happy • Good • Clean • Calm

☺

COMBING/BRUSHING YOUR HAIR
Behaviors That Are **UNEXPECTED**

Behaviors, feelings, and consequences are listed in categories in arbitrary order. There is not a one-to-one correlation between the information listed in each column. For example, whatever behavior is listed first does not have to match to the first emotional reaction or the first consequence, and so on.

Unexpected Behaviors You Produce	How They Make Others Feel	Consequences You Experience	How You Feel About Yourself
• Not combing or brushing hair. • Combing or brushing hair while at the dinner table. • Combing/brushing hair around food. • Not combing hair after you wash your hair, leaving it tangled. • Taking off your hat and not combing your hair down. • Sharing combs or brushes with others. • Combing/brushing hair in public.	• Surprised • Grossed out • Embarrassed • Disgusted	• Your parents will nag you to comb your hair. • People will laugh at you. • People will yell at you. • People are disgusted if hair is in your food. • People will say your hair looks messy. • People might laugh at your funny looking hair. • You could spread germs. • People might have weird thoughts about you.	• Mad • Embarrassed • Sad • Upset • Messy

→

→

DEALING WITH YOUR PERIOD
Behaviors That Are **EXPECTED**

Behaviors, feelings, and consequences are listed in categories in arbitrary order. There is not a one-to-one correlation between the information listed in each column. For example, whatever behavior is listed first does not have to match to the first emotional reaction or the first consequence, and so on.

Expected Behaviors You Produce	How They Make Others Feel	Consequences You Experience	How You Feel About Yourself
• Plan ahead. Know what day you are expected to start your period. • Be prepared. Have tampons or sanitary napkins with you in your purse or backpack. • If you think you might be bleeding without protection, and you are in a group of people, simply get up, say, "excuse me," and go to the bathroom to check yourself. • If you don't have a tampon or napkin, ask another girl for them by whispering the question, "Can I borrow a tampon?" • Go to the restroom and change your napkin or tampon often on the first days of your period. This could be every two hours. • Do not announce to everyone what your intentions are. This is a personal and private matter. • Wrap the tampon or napkin in toilet paper and place it in the waste container. • Mark on a calendar the first day of your cycle and the last day of your cycle to help you be prepared for next time. • Change your pants if you bleed through them. You may need to call home for clean pants, or tie a sweatshirt around your waist, to hide the stain. • Change your underwear daily.	• Pleased • Comfortable • Thankful • Respected → ☺	• You will not be surprised. • You will not have to ask others if they have a napkin or tampon that you could have. You will not get your clothes messy. • Nobody but you will know. • You will feel clean and sanitary. • People will have respect for you. • Others will not get mad and yell because the toilet is backed up. • You will know when your cycle will start next month and approximately how long it will be. →	• Good • Clean • Calm • Responsible

DEALING WITH YOUR PERIOD
Behaviors That Are **UNEXPECTED**

Behaviors, feelings, and consequences are listed in categories in arbitrary order. There is not a one-to-one correlation between the information listed in each column. For example, whatever behavior is listed first does not have to match to the first emotional reaction or the first consequence, and so on.

Unexpected Behaviors You Produce	How They Make Others Feel	Consequences You Experience	How You Feel About Yourself
• Not having a clue that your cycle is due. • Not being prepared. Do not have any tampons or napkins. • If in a group of people, getting up and announcing that you have started your period. • Loudly asking people if they have a tampon or napkin. • Not bothering to go and check yourself. • Not putting on a sanitary napkin (or tampon). • Not marking on a calendar when your cycle began and ended. • If you bleed through your pants, you don't change them. • Don't change your underwear if you are using a napkin.	• Surprised • Annoyed • Grossed out • Embarrassed • Disgusted	• You freak out. • You have to ask others for a tampon, or call your home. • Others have weird thoughts about you because people are not supposed to know you have your period. • You get blood on your clothes. • Next month it happens again and you are not prepared again.	• Scared • Embarrassed • Bad • Upset • Messy

FLOSSING YOUR TEETH
Behaviors That Are **EXPECTED**

Behaviors, feelings, and consequences are listed in categories in arbitrary order. There is not a one-to-one correlation between the information listed in each column. For example, whatever behavior is listed first does not have to match to the first emotional reaction or the first consequence, and so on.

Expected Behaviors You Produce	How They Make Others Feel	Consequences You Experience	How You Feel About Yourself
• Floss your teeth daily. • Floss your teeth in privacy. • If you floss in front of a mirror, wipe off the mirror when finished. • Use fresh floss every time you floss. • Throw away the used floss in the garbage. • Use floss only for flossing your teeth.	• Happy • Grateful • Pleased	• Your parents smile and say they are proud of you. • Others do not think your teeth are gross. • Your parents do not nag or yell at you to throw away your floss. • Your gums stay healthy.	• Good • Clean • Happy

→

→

☺

FLOSSING YOUR TEETH
Behaviors That Are **UNEXPECTED**

Behaviors, feelings, and consequences are listed in categories in arbitrary order. There is not a one-to-one correlation between the information listed in each column. For example, whatever behavior is listed first does not have to match to the first emotional reaction or the first consequence, and so on.

Unexpected Behaviors You Produce	How They Make Others Feel	Consequences You Experience	How You Feel About Yourself
• Not flossing daily. • Flossing your teeth in public. • Floss in front of mirror and getting gross teeth gunk on mirror, then not wiping it off. • Continue using the same piece of floss you used already. • Leaving used floss all over the bathroom. • Using floss for things that it was not intended for.	• Grossed out • Angry • Disgusted • Surprised	• You get cavities and gum disease. • People do not want to be around you. • Your parents nag and yell at you to clean the mirror and throw away your floss. • Your parents tell you that what you are doing is not sanitary.	• Upset • Embarrassed • Anxious • Unhappy

→

→

USING THE TOILET
Behaviors That Are **EXPECTED**

Behaviors, feelings, and consequences are listed in categories in arbitrary order. There is not a one-to-one correlation between the information listed in each column. For example, whatever behavior is listed first does not have to match to the first emotional reaction or the first consequence, and so on.

Expected Behaviors You Produce	How They Make Others Feel	Consequences You Experience	How You Feel About Yourself
• If you're in a group of people, simply say excuse me and then go to the restroom. • Lifting the toilet seat (if you're a boy). • Urinating only IN the toilet. • Covering the seat if you have to sit down (if you are in a public restroom). • When finished, putting the seat back down. • Washing hands when finished. • Drying hands after washing. • Returning directly if others are waiting for you.	• Happy • Grateful • Pleased →	• Others smile and excuse you. • Others do not yell at you because you got the seat wet. • Your parents will not nag you to stop urinating on the floor. • Your mom (and sister) will not complain that the seat is always up. • You are safe. • You will reduce the chances of getting sick. • Others will not think it's gross because your hands are wet. • Others will not get angry about waiting and come looking for you. → ☺	• Good • Clean • Happy

USING THE TOILET
Behaviors That Are **UNEXPECTED**

Behaviors, feelings, and consequences are listed in categories in arbitrary order. There is not a one-to-one correlation between the information listed in each column. For example, whatever behavior is listed first does not have to match to the first emotional reaction or the first consequence, and so on.

Unexpected Behaviors You Produce	How They Make Others Feel	Consequences You Experience	How You Feel About Yourself
• Jumping up and down and yelling that you have to go to the bathroom. • Not lifting the toilet seat (If you are a boy). • Urinating all around the toilet, including the floor and seat. • If you are in a public restroom and you have to sit, not covering the seat. • Leaving the toilet seat up. • Not washing your hands. • Not drying your hands. • Staying in the restroom for a long time.	• Grossed out • Annoyed • Disgusted • Surprised →	• People yell at you to GO. • People yell at you because you got the seat wet. • Your parent nags you to cover the seat because it is not sanitary. • You might get sick. • Others look at you weird. • Others come looking for you. →	• Upset • Embarrassed • Anxious • Unhappy • Confused

USING THE URINAL
Behaviors That Are **EXPECTED**

Behaviors, feelings, and consequences are listed in categories in arbitrary order. There is not a one-to-one correlation between the information listed in each column. For example, whatever behavior is listed first does not have to match to the first emotional reaction or the first consequence, and so on.

Expected Behaviors You Produce	How They Make Others Feel	Consequences You Experience	How You Feel About Yourself
• Walk up to a urinal not being used by others. • Stare straight ahead or look down at your pants in order to get yourself ready to urinate. • Keep your voice quiet. • Urinate directly into the urinal. • Zip your pants back up. • Wash your hands. • As soon as you are done with your business, walk out of the bathroom.	• Calm • Comfortable • Relieved →	• You will feel more comfortable. • People will not talk to you but they also will not have weird thoughts about you. • Your washed hands will keep germs from spreading. →	• Calm • Comfortable • Relieved

☺

USING THE URINAL
Behaviors That Are **UNEXPECTED**

Behaviors, feelings, and consequences are listed in categories in arbitrary order. There is not a one-to-one correlation between the information listed in each column. For example, whatever behavior is listed first does not have to match to the first emotional reaction or the first consequence, and so on.

Unexpected Behaviors You Produce	How They Make Others Feel	Consequences You Experience	How You Feel About Yourself
• Tell people to move when they are using the urinal. • Talk to other boys while they are urinating. • Touch other boys while they are urinating. • Looking at other boys' penises while they are urinating. • Not zipping up your pants. • Not washing your hands. • Masturbating or touching your penis other than to urinate. • Staying in the bathroom and playing with the water.	• Frustrated • Insulted • Angry • Stressed • Grossed out →	• People will tell you to be quiet. • People will tell you you are gross. • A boy might push you away. • People tell you to get out of the bathroom. • You spread germs or give yourself bad germs. →	• Frustrated • Embarrassed • Mad • Uncomfortable

WASHING YOUR HAIR
Behaviors That Are **EXPECTED**

Behaviors, feelings, and consequences are listed in categories in arbitrary order. There is not a one-to-one correlation between the information listed in each column. For example, whatever behavior is listed first does not have to match to the first emotional reaction or the first consequence, and so on.

Expected Behaviors You Produce	How They Make Others Feel	Consequences You Experience	How You Feel About Yourself
• Wash hair daily once you are in puberty. • Wet your entire head of hair. • Put a dollop of shampoo on your hand and rub your hands together. • Soap your entire head of hair with shampoo. • Rinse shampoo out of your hair. • If you have dandruff, use a dandruff shampoo. • After shampooing, use a conditioner to make your hair easy to comb. • Rinse the conditioner thoroughly out of your hair. • Dry your hair, first by rubbing a towel through it. • Comb your hair.	• Happy • Impressed • Pleased →	• Your hair will look clean and shiny. • You won't have dandruff. • People will not think you are dirty or smelly. • Your hair is easy to comb while it is wet. • Your hair will look good. →	• Good • Clean • Happy

☺

WASHING YOUR HAIR
Behaviors That Are **UNEXPECTED**

Behaviors, feelings, and consequences are listed in categories in arbitrary order. There is not a one-to-one correlation between the information listed in each column. For example, whatever behavior is listed first does not have to match to the first emotional reaction or the first consequence, and so on.

Unexpected Behaviors You Produce	How They Make Others Feel	Consequences You Experience	How You Feel About Yourself
• Not washing your hair daily. • Wetting only the top of your head. • Applying shampoo to only the top of your head. • Not using dandruff shampoo if you need it. • Not rinsing all of the shampoo from your hair. • Not using conditioner. • Not drying your hair. • Not combing your hair. • Crying because you hate water on your head. • Telling people that no one notices if your hair is dirty. • Refusing to wash your hair.	• Grossed out • Annoyed • Disgusted • Surprised →	• People do not want to be around you. • Your parent tells you to go back and do it again. • People will laugh and make fun of your dandruff problem. • People will think you look messy or dirty in an uncool way. →	• Upset • Embarrassed • Anxious • Unhappy

☹

WEARING DEODORANT
Behaviors That Are **EXPECTED**

Behaviors, feelings, and consequences are listed in categories in arbitrary order. There is not a one-to-one correlation between the information listed in each column. For example, whatever behavior is listed first does not have to match to the first emotional reaction or the first consequence, and so on.

Expected Behaviors You Produce	How They Make Others Feel	Consequences You Experience	How You Feel About Yourself
• Apply every morning after your shower. • Do not apply too much – it might get all over your clothes. • Apply in the privacy of your bathroom or bedroom. • Do not apply in public. • Apply only to your armpits. • If you are running out, be sure to buy more before you are totally out.	• Happy • Grateful • Thankful →	• You will smell fresh, and others will like that. • You will look good, and others will enjoy that. • People will not make fun of you for smelling bad. • People will not make fun of you for applying it in public. • You will not be caught without deodorant. →	• Good • Clean • Fresh

WEARING DEODORANT
Behaviors That Are **UNEXPECTED**

Behaviors, feelings, and consequences are listed in categories in arbitrary order. There is not a one-to-one correlation between the information listed in each column. For example, whatever behavior is listed first does not have to match to the first emotional reaction or the first consequence, and so on.

Unexpected Behaviors You Produce	How They Make Others Feel	Consequences You Experience	How You Feel About Yourself
• Not applying daily. • Applying too much and getting it all over your clothing. • Applying in public. • Applying to areas not intended for use. • Running out.	• Grossed out • Annoyed • Disgusted • Surprised	• People tell you that you stink. • People point and laugh because you have deodorant all over your clothes. • People say that you are gross. • You stink because you ran out of deodorant.	• Upset • Embarrassed • Anxious • Lonely

→

→

APPLYING MAKEUP
Behaviors That Are **EXPECTED**

Behaviors, feelings, and consequences are listed in categories in arbitrary order. There is not a one-to-one correlation between the information listed in each column. For example, whatever behavior is listed first does not have to match to the first emotional reaction or the first consequence, and so on.

Expected Behaviors You Produce	How They Make Others Feel	Consequences You Experience	How You Feel About Yourself
• Look your age. • Wear minimal makeup. • Wear only with your parents' permission. • Never share your makeup. • Do not apply in public. • Do not over-buy makeup. • Ask peers for advice if you like how they wear their makeup.	• Pleased • Proud • Happy →	• Others smile at you. • Your parents will not nag you to take your makeup off. • Your parents will not yell at you. • You and your friends will not get an infection. • Others will have good thoughts about you. • Your parents will not yell at you and tell you to stop spending all of your money on makeup. →	• Happy • Proud • Pleased • Attractive

☺

APPLYING MAKEUP
Behaviors That Are **UNEXPECTED**

Behaviors, feelings, and consequences are listed in categories in arbitrary order. There is not a one-to-one correlation between the information listed in each column. For example, whatever behavior is listed first does not have to match to the first emotional reaction or the first consequence, and so on.

Unexpected Behaviors You Produce	How They Make Others Feel	Consequences You Experience	How You Feel About Yourself
• Trying to look older. • Wearing too much makeup. • Sneaking around to put makeup on without your parents' permission. • Sharing makeup. • Applying makeup in public. • Spending all of your money on makeup.	• Embarrassed • Scared • Grossed out • Surprised • Frustrated	• Others stare at you. • Others laugh at you. • Your parents may ground you. • You could get an infection due to sharing makeup. • People think you are vain. • You never have any money.	• Embarrassed • Sad • Lonely • Frustrated

→

→

MEALTIME WITH FAMILY
Behaviors That Are **EXPECTED**

Behaviors, feelings, and consequences are listed in categories in arbitrary order. There is not a one-to-one correlation between the information listed in each column. For example, whatever behavior is listed first does not have to match to the first emotional reaction or the first consequence, and so on.

Expected Behaviors You Produce	How They Make Others Feel	Consequences You Experience	How You Feel About Yourself
• Keep your mouth closed while eating. • Talk AFTER you swallow food. • Use an inside voice. • Take turns talking. • Keep your elbows off the table. • Keep your hands in your lap. • Take quiet gulps when drinking. • Ask questions about other people's day. • Sit in your chair calmly without fidgeting. • Use silverware appropriately. • Place your fork and knife at 4 o'clock position on your plate while chewing and when you have finished your meal. • Take appropriate portions. • Look with your eyes at the person talking to you. • Be polite—ask to be excused when you are finished.	• Calm and able to enjoy meal • Happy • Proud • Confident • Impressed →	• Others compliment you on what a great job you are doing. • The family looks forward to your next meal together. • Others can share ideas as part of the family. • You may get to go to restaurants. • Enjoy the meal. →	• Proud • Happy • Calm

☺

MEALTIME WITH FAMILY
Behaviors That Are **UNEXPECTED**

Behaviors, feelings, and consequences are listed in categories in arbitrary order. There is not a one-to-one correlation between the information listed in each column. For example, whatever behavior is listed first does not have to match to the first emotional reaction or the first consequence, and so on.

Unexpected Behaviors You Produce	How They Make Others Feel	Consequences You Experience	How You Feel About Yourself
• Chewing with your mouth full and open. • Chewing too loudly. • Using a loud voice. • Interrupting. • Touching/playing with silverware. • Slurping drinks. • Talking only about what you want to talk about. • Not talking at all. • Fidgeting, standing, touching others.	• Embarrassed • Frustrated • Stressed • Sad that you are not interested in other family members • Worried • Concerned about whether you are okay – is something wrong?	• Your parents nag and tell you how to act. • Your parents ask you to leave the table. • Others will have weird thoughts about you, or think you are not polite. • Others will ask you to stop talking or let others talk. • Others wonder if they can take you to restaurants. • People will not enjoy their meal.	• Frustrated • Tired • Annoyed • Lonely • Uncomfortable

→

→

SHARING WITH SIBLINGS
Behaviors That Are EXPECTED

Behaviors, feelings, and consequences are listed in categories in arbitrary order. There is not a one-to-one correlation between the information listed in each column. For example, whatever behavior is listed first does not have to match to the first emotional reaction or the first consequence, and so on.

Expected Behaviors You Produce	How They Make Others Feel	Consequences You Experience	How You Feel About Yourself
• Whole body is calm and listening. • Listen to a "sharing request" from your brother or sister ("Can I play with _____?"). • Agree to let your brother or sister share your toys or items that you are using or that belong to you. • May politely provide any special rules you have about using your items (e.g., Sure, but please don't use the erasers on my colored pencils). • When they return them, politely say, "Thank you."	• Happy • Proud • Relaxed/calm • Relieved	• Your parents may compliment you on how well you are getting along with your brother or sister. • Your brother or sister will also want to share their items with you. • Your house is a calm place to live and everyone feels comfortable. • Your toys or items you are sharing will stay in good condition. • Family members will have good thoughts about you.	• Happy • Proud • Calm

→

→

☺

SHARING WITH SIBLINGS
Behaviors That Are **UNEXPECTED**

Behaviors, feelings, and consequences are listed in categories in arbitrary order. There is not a one-to-one correlation between the information listed in each column. For example, whatever behavior is listed first does not have to match to the first emotional reaction or the first consequence, and so on.

Unexpected Behaviors You Produce	How They Make Others Feel	Consequences You Experience	How You Feel About Yourself
• Body is turned away from your brother or sister. • Not thinking about your brother or sister with your eyes while they are making a "sharing request." • Refuse to share your toys or items with your brother or sister. • Use mean words or voice to respond to your brother or sister. • If you share the item, give them a long list of rules to follow.	• Sad • Frustrated • Tense • Hurt • Overwhelmed	• Your parent may have to come over and nag you to share with your brother or sister. • Now you may not have any say in the decision! • Your brother or sister will remember this and will not want to share with you. • People have not-so-good thoughts about you. • Your brother or sister may not follow all of your rules because you gave so many to follow. • Household is tense because siblings are not getting along. • May escalate into an argument and someone may be sent to her room.	• Frustrated • Tired • Annoyed • Uncomfortable • Tense

DOING CHORES
Behaviors That Are EXPECTED

Behaviors, feelings, and consequences are listed in categories in arbitrary order. There is not a one-to-one correlation between the information listed in each column. For example, whatever behavior is listed first does not have to match to the first emotional reaction or the first consequence, and so on.

Expected Behaviors You Produce	How They Make Others Feel	Consequences You Experience	How You Feel About Yourself
• Without anyone reminding you, complete your weekly chores. • If reminded to do your chore, say, "Okay" and immediately stop what you are doing and start on your chore. • Stay focused on the chore until it is done. • Take your time and do a thorough job.	• Happy • Proud • Relaxed/calm • Relieved →	• The house will look clean if everyone is pitching in and doing their job. • Compliment you on your great job! • Family members will have good thoughts about you. • May get allowance. • May be allowed to go out and play or out with friends. • You will have more time to play or do what you want to do if the chore is done right the first time. • Parents will continue to help you (e.g., doing your laundry as part of their chore). →	• Happy • Proud • Calm

DOING CHORES
Behaviors That Are **UNEXPECTED**

Behaviors, feelings, and consequences are listed in categories in arbitrary order. There is not a one-to-one correlation between the information listed in each column. For example, whatever behavior is listed first does not have to match to the first emotional reaction or the first consequence, and so on.

Unexpected Behaviors You Produce	How They Make Others Feel	Consequences You Experience	How You Feel About Yourself
• When reminded about chores, say "no" or "I will get to it later." • Make disrespectful comments or yell when your parents remind you to do your chore. • Choose to play or do what you want to do when it is chore time. • Start the chore and then get distracted with something else that you want to do. • Tell your parent you did your chore when you did not. • Spend only a few minutes or rush through your chore. • Leave the house when you know you are expected to do a chore. • Get your sibling to do your chore.	• Upset • Frustrated • Tense • Hurt • Stressed	• Not doing the chore will make the house look dirty or untidy. • Family members will think you are lazy or irresponsible. • Parents may have to nag and ask you to do your chore. • Family members may decide to stop helping you out (e.g., doing your laundry), if you do not work as part of the family. • May lose allowance or your parents may say no to your requests for money during the week. • Parents may ground you. • Parents may ask you to do the chore over until it is done right.	• Frustrated • Tired • Annoyed • Uncomfortable • Tense

WATCHING TV WITH YOUR FAMILY
Behaviors That Are **EXPECTED**

Behaviors, feelings, and consequences are listed in categories in arbitrary order. There is not a one-to-one correlation between the information listed in each column. For example, whatever behavior is listed first does not have to match to the first emotional reaction or the first consequence, and so on.

Expected Behaviors You Produce	How They Make Others Feel	Consequences You Experience	How You Feel About Yourself
• Listen to what shows or movies others want to watch. • Compromise to find something everyone will want to watch. • Stay quiet while the show is on. • If someone is already watching a show or movie, walk in quietly, sit down and watch if you want to watch the show. • Talk during commercials or before the movie starts. • Keep "it's boring" thoughts to yourself.	• Happy • Calm • Relaxed →	• The family will get to enjoy TV and time together. • Family members will want to watch more TV with you. • You may get to pick the show to watch next time. • After the show is over, they may ask you what you want to watch. • Parents may compliment you on being flexible. →	• Relaxed • Happy

☺

WATCHING TV WITH YOUR FAMILY
Behaviors That Are **UNEXPECTED**

Behaviors, feelings, and consequences are listed in categories in arbitrary order. There is not a one-to-one correlation between the information listed in each column. For example, whatever behavior is listed first does not have to match to the first emotional reaction or the first consequence, and so on.

Unexpected Behaviors You Produce	How They Make Others Feel	Consequences You Experience	How You Feel About Yourself
• Only suggest what you want to watch. • Fidget, invade space on furniture. • Talk during the show. • Tell others what will happen next. • Insist that everyone watch only your show. • Say "this is boring" or "I want to watch something else." • Grab the remote control and change the channel at any time you want.	• Annoyed • Angry • Frustrated • Upset • Nervous	• Others will feel uncomfortable and may ask you to move away. • Parents will ask you to be quiet. • Others will tell you to leave and find something else to do. • Others will not give you a choice of show next time. • Others will not want to watch TV with you again. • People yell at you.	• Hurt • Annoyed • Rejected • Sad

→

→

☹

 # A FAMILY MEETING
Behaviors That Are **EXPECTED**

Behaviors, feelings, and consequences are listed in categories in arbitrary order. There is not a one-to-one correlation between the information listed in each column. For example, whatever behavior is listed first does not have to match to the first emotional reaction or the first consequence, and so on.

Expected Behaviors You Produce	How They Make Others Feel	Consequences You Experience	How You Feel About Yourself
• Sitting calmly and listening with your whole body. • Raise your hand if you have a question or wait until the person is done talking. • Add comments or ideas that are on topic. • Keep your information short (1-2 sentences). • Being flexible with new rules or changes in the household.	• Happy • Proud • Relaxed/calm • Relieved	• Meeting will get done faster. • Parents may compliment you for doing a great job. • May get a reward or treat. • Family members can solve problems as a team and everyone will get a chance to share their ideas. • May have time to play or do something that you want to do before bedtime.	• Happy • Proud • Calm

→

→

☺

A FAMILY MEETING
Behaviors That Are UN**EXPECTED**

Behaviors, feelings, and consequences are listed in categories in arbitrary order. There is not a one-to-one correlation between the information listed in each column. For example, whatever behavior is listed first does not have to match to the first emotional reaction or the first consequence, and so on.

Unexpected Behaviors You Produce	How They Make Others Feel	Consequences You Experience	How You Feel About Yourself
• Fidgeting in your chair. • Using a loud (outside) voice. • Interrupting or blurting out your ideas. • Criticizing others' ideas or comments during the meeting. • Repeatedly going back to a topic you want to talk about because you are not happy with the outcome. • Dominating the meeting and doing most of the talking. • Insisting things be done your way or not being flexible with others' ideas.	• Frustrated • Annoyed • Hurt/sad • Bored • Disinterested • Stressed →	• Parents may use their nagging voice. • You may be asked to sit away from the meeting until it is done. • Parents may ask you to apologize for your comments. • Meeting may take longer. • May not be able to get through all the items for the family meeting. • May not get to talk about the meeting items that relate to you. →	• Frustrated • Annoyed • Sad • Tense

WHEN YOU NEED HELP
BUT MOM AND DAD ARE BUSY
Behaviors That Are **EXPECTED**

Behaviors, feelings, and consequences are listed in categories in arbitrary order. There is not a one-to-one correlation between the information listed in each column. For example, whatever behavior is listed first does not have to match to the first emotional reaction or the first consequence, and so on.

Expected Behaviors You Produce	How They Make Others Feel	Consequences You Experience	How You Feel About Yourself
• Body is calm. • Use an inside voice. • Decide who you will ask for help and read their plan (what are they doing?). Is now a good time to interrupt? • If your parents look busy, quietly move your body next to them so they can see you. • Calmly ask them if they can help you when they are done. • If they are on the phone, wait until they are off the phone to get their help. • If a parent is on the phone and you need to get his help for a big problem, calmly take your body next to him and wait until he looks at you and asks you what you need.	• Happy • Proud • Relaxed/calm • Relieved →	• You will get the help you need. • Your parents may compliment you or thank you for waiting patiently. • They may stop what they are doing to help you. • Your parents were able to finish what they were working on. →	• Happy • Proud • Calm

☺

WHEN YOU NEED HELP
BUT MOM AND DAD ARE BUSY
Behaviors That Are UNEXPECTED

Behaviors, feelings, and consequences are listed in categories in arbitrary order. There is not a one-to-one correlation between the information listed in each column. For example, whatever behavior is listed first does not have to match to the first emotional reaction or the first consequence, and so on.

Unexpected Behaviors You Produce	How They Make Others Feel	Consequences You Experience	How You Feel About Yourself
• Tug or pull on their clothes to get their attention. • Keep repeating or yelling their name. • Walk up and tell them what is wrong without thinking about what they are busy doing. • Interrupting while a parent is on the phone. • Body is hyper and jumping around.	• Frustrated • Annoyed • Stressed	• Your parents may yell or use a mad tone to ask you to wait. • Your parents may nag and remind you to wait until they are finished. • You may have to wait longer for help.	• Frustrated • Annoyed • Sad • Tense • Embarrassed

BEDTIME
Behaviors That Are **EXPECTED**

Behaviors, feelings, and consequences are listed in categories in arbitrary order. There is not a one-to-one correlation between the information listed in each column. For example, whatever behavior is listed first does not have to match to the first emotional reaction or the first consequence, and so on.

Expected Behaviors You Produce	How They Make Others Feel	Consequences You Experience	How You Feel About Yourself
• Drink your bedtime drink before brushing teeth. • Respond with "okay" and walk toward room. • Use an inside voice. • Stop whatever you are doing and get started preparing for bed. • Change into pajamas. • Get into bed and sleep.	• Happy • Proud • Relaxed/calm • Relieved	• You will get enough sleep for school. • Parents will compliment you. • Family members will have good thoughts about you. • Parents will think you are responsible. • Parents may let you stay up longer another night if you show responsibility.	• Happy • Proud • Energized the next day

→

→

🙂

BEDTIME
Behaviors That Are **UNEXPECTED**

Behaviors, feelings, and consequences are listed in categories in arbitrary order. There is not a one-to-one correlation between the information listed in each column. For example, whatever behavior is listed first does not have to match to the first emotional reaction or the first consequence, and so on.

Unexpected Behaviors You Produce	How They Make Others Feel	Consequences You Experience	How You Feel About Yourself
• Not brushing your teeth. • Playing video games, reading, or playing with toys during bedtime routine. • Using an outside voice. • Telling your parents you are doing something else. • Sleeping in your clothes.	• Frustrated • Worried • Angry • Stressed • Upset	• You will get cavities. • You will not get enough sleep. • You will lose privileges. • Your parents nag and tell you to get ready for bed. • You look unkempt.	• Frustrated • Tired • Annoyed • Uncomfortable

BEING WITH MOM ALL SUMMER
Behaviors That Are **EXPECTED**

Behaviors, feelings, and consequences are listed in categories in arbitrary order. There is not a one-to-one correlation between the information listed in each column. For example, whatever behavior is listed first does not have to match to the first emotional reaction or the first consequence, and so on.

Expected Behaviors You Produce	How They Make Others Feel	Consequences You Experience	How You Feel About Yourself

• Nice:
  • Use friendly words
  • Show interest in her
  • Say "please" and "thank you"
  • Give her a compliment
 	
• Smile at her.
 	
• Look at her when talking to her.
 	
• Have your body be alert; do not slump over at the table when you are with her.
 	
• Follow directions.
 	
• Anticipate what she wants you to do before she asks you!
	• Good
	• Happy
	• Proud
	• Thrilled
		• She compliments you.
		
		• She does something nice for you.
		
		• She returns nice words, a nice tone of voice, a smile, back to you!
			• Good
			• Proud
			• Relaxed

→ → ☺

BEING WITH MOM ALL SUMMER
Behaviors That Are **UNEXPECTED**

Behaviors, feelings, and consequences are listed in categories in arbitrary order. There is not a one-to-one correlation between the information listed in each column. For example, whatever behavior is listed first does not have to match to the first emotional reaction or the first consequence, and so on.

Unexpected Behaviors You Produce	How They Make Others Feel	Consequences You Experience	How You Feel About Yourself

• Not Being Nice:
  • Unfriendly words
  • Don't show interest in her
  • Don't say "please" or "thank you"
  • Rude remarks
 	
• Flat facial expression (not smiling).
 	
• Not looking at her.
 	
• Body always slumping.
 	
• Not following directions.
 	
• Not anticipating what she wants you to do, so you don't do anything to help.
	• Bad
	
	• Frustrated
	
	• Angry
	
	• Worried you won't ever get along with others
		• She nags you to use more skills.
		
		• She yells!
		
		• She leaves the house to get a break from her frustration.
		
		• No special treats.
			• Bad
			
			• Angry
			
			• Frustrated
			
			• Lonely

→

→

☹

SocialThinking® has so much to offer!

OUR MISSION

At Social Thinking, our mission is to help people develop their social competencies to better connect with others and experience deeper well-being. We create unique treatment frameworks and strategies to help individuals develop their social thinking and related social skills to meet their academic, personal and professional social goals. These goals often include sharing space effectively with others, learning to work as part of a team, and developing relationships of all kinds: with family, friends, classmates, co-workers, romantic partners, etc.

ARTICLES

100+ free educational articles and treatment strategies

CONFERENCES, eLEARNING & CUSTOM TRAINING

Courses and embedded training for schools and organizations

PRODUCTS

Books, games, posters, music and more!

CLINICAL RESEARCH

Measuring the effectiveness of the Social Thinking Methodology

TREATMENT: CHILDREN & ADULTS

Clinical treatment, assessments, school consultations, etc.

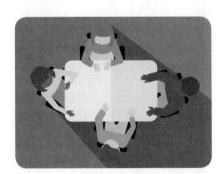

CLINICAL TRAINING PROGRAM

Three-day intensive training for professionals